CW00959912

10-MINUTE

CRYSTAL BALL

Easy Tips for Developing Your Inner
Wisdom and Psychic Powers

WRITTEN BY

SKYE ALEXANDER

Brimming with creative inspiration, how-to projects, and useful information to enrich your everyday life, Quarto Knows is a favorite destination for those pursuing their interests and passions. Visit our site and dig deeper with our books into your area of interest: Quarto Creates, Quarto Cooks, Quarto Homes, Quarto Lives, Quarto Drives, Quarto Explores, Quarto Gifts, or Quarto Kids.

© 2019 Quarto Publishing Group USA Inc.
Text © 2002, 2019 by Skye Alexander

First Published in 2002 by Fair Winds Press, an imprint of The Quarto Group,
100 Cummings Center, Suite 265-D, Beverly, MA 01915, USA.
T (978) 282-9590 F (978) 283-2742 QuartoKnows.com

All rights reserved. No part of this book may be reproduced in any form without written permission of the copyright owners. All images in this book have been reproduced with the knowledge and prior consent of the artists concerned, and no responsibility is accepted by producer, publisher, or printer for any infringement of copyright or otherwise, arising from the contents of this publication. Every effort has been made to ensure that credits accurately comply with information supplied. We apologize for any inaccuracies that may have occurred and will resolve inaccurate or missing information in a subsequent reprinting of the book.

Fair Winds Press titles are also available at discount for retail, wholesale, promotional, and bulk purchase. For details, contact the Special Sales Manager by email at specialsales@quarto.com or by mail at The Quarto Group, Attn: Special Sales Manager, 100 Cummings Center, 265-D, Beverly, MA 01915, USA.

23 22 21 20 19   1 2 3 4 5

ISBN: 978-1-59233-881-8

Digital edition published in 2019
eISBN: 978-1-63159-706-0

Library of Congress Cataloging-in-Publication Data found under *10-Minute Crystal Ball*.

Design, page layout, and illustrations: Tanya Jacobson, crsld.co

Printed in China

TO MY MOTHER, WHO
ENCOURAGED ME TO DEVELOP
MY PSYCHIC ABILITY

Contents

Introduction

Think about how much you'd miss out on if you lacked vision, or hearing, or the ability to taste. Without one of your five physical senses, you'd have a much harder time coping with the challenges of daily life. Your world would be duller and more hazardous; your opportunities and experiences would diminish.

Now imagine how much more you might be able to achieve and enjoy if you had another sense. What new possibilities would come within your reach? What doors would open to you?

Actually, you do have a "sixth sense." Everybody does. Most of us just don't use it. This untapped resource—your psychic power—is a natural, readily available ability that can increase your appreciation of the world around you, enrich your interactions with other people, and help you create the life you want.

Due to lack of use, your "psychic muscles" have probably atrophied. But like your biceps or abs, they can be strengthened with a bit of exercise. *10-Minute Crystal Ball* contains lots of easy, fun exercises to develop your psychic skills and help you become a winner in the marathon of life.

How to Use This Book

Most of us have neither the time nor the desire to hole up in an ashram for an extended period of time or embark on a lengthy apprenticeship with a spiritual master in order to reach a higher state of consciousness. *10-Minute Crystal Ball* is designed for practical, busy people who want to improve their psychic skills and use them more effectively in their daily lives.

Most of the tips and exercises in Part Two can be done in ten minutes or less, and I recommend practicing at least some of them on a regular basis. Psychic ability is like any other skill—the more you use it, the sharper it becomes. If you aren't interested in learning the basics about psychic powers or how they operate, go directly to this section and get started.

For those of you who are curious about the philosophy and methodology behind the results, Part One covers the fundamentals of psychic phenomena without getting too technical or mystical. This section also explains some of the tools employed by seers, magicians, and other "frequent fliers" in the psychic realm.

There's nothing peculiar or scary about psychic ability—we all possess it. Once you grow accustomed to using your sixth sense, you'll realize that it is as normal as your other five senses—and just as valuable.

PART ONE

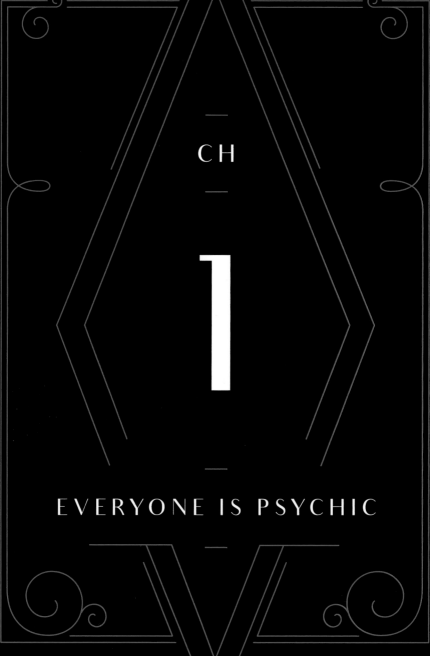

CH

1

EVERYONE IS PSYCHIC

W hat image comes to mind when you hear the word psychic? Someone in a turban hunched over a crystal ball? An aged mystic chanting strange words?

Actually, we all possess psychic ability. Hunch, gut feeling, intuition— these are words we use to describe an inner guidance that surfaces in our everyday waking consciousness and slips us information we couldn't have gotten through the usual sensory channels. Many police officers and nurses are familiar with this sort of "inner knowing"—their own lives or the lives entrusted to them may depend on these professionals paying attention to their intuition. Some successful investors rely not only on practical data but also on their "feelings" about particular stocks. And mothers often display an uncanny knowledge of circumstances their children face, particularly with regard to matters of health and safety.

Sir Winston Churchill, Britain's prime minister during World War II, was guided by his sixth sense throughout his lifetime. Once, during a dinner party, he had a feeling that his guests and staff should head for the bomb shelter. Moments later, a bomb hit his home—but thanks to Churchill's premonition, everyone was safe.

Most people are either skeptical of or suspicious about psychic ability, or they reject it altogether. Modern Western society has a rational/logical bias that discounts what can't be explained in quantifiable, physical terms. Young children frequently experience visions, voices, premonitions, and other psychic events—until their elders admonish them for talking about them. By the time we're in our teens, we've learned to keep the lid on any "weird stuff" for fear of being ridiculed, or worse. We turn down the volume on our psychic receivers and usually ignore their gentle promptings.

Yet it's the rare individual who hasn't had a brush with the psychic realm. The media are full of stories about people who at the last minute didn't board a plane that later crashed, felt an inexplicable urge to go to a certain place and met their true love there, bought lottery tickets on a hunch and won the jackpot. Although you may not have experienced anything quite so dramatic, you've undoubtedly been thinking something just as another person says it aloud, or received a phone call from someone you'd just been thinking about. This type of mental telepathy is the most common form of psychic event. Are these just coincidences? Or is there something more to it?

THE PSYCHIC REALM

Some researchers believe that psychic ability is really a matter of pattern recognition—a person subconsciously observes and pieces together repeated symbols, experiences, or behavior, such as body language, to "read" someone else's mind or to anticipate events. Another theory proposes that stored memories—a picture glimpsed long ago in a book or a conversation overheard in childhood—are the sources for knowledge that seems to come out of nowhere. But while pattern recognition and stored memories may explain some incidents, they can't account for all psychic phenomena.

The concept I prefer suggests that a nonphysical energy field surrounds and permeates all matter, connecting us to each other and to the whole of existence. It's a little like the Internet, which links us electronically to people everywhere via the World Wide Web, except this energetic "cosmic web" is far more elegant. This network contains information in its entirety, and everyone can access it with the right password. Swiss psychiatrist C. G. Jung called this energy network the *collective unconscious*. The Austrian mystic Rudolf Steiner referred to it as the *etheric realm*.

Many people find it easier to access the psychic realm when they are asleep or in an altered state of consciousness, as during meditation or hypnosis. Illness, too, can dissolve the barriers to intuition. It seems that when we loosen our grasp on our rational, analytical thinking processes and allow our minds to float freely, the doors of perception open to admit all sorts of impressions and impulses that we ordinarily block.

Edgar Cayce is probably the best-known psychic of our age. Called the Sleeping Prophet, Cayce could freely navigate the psychic realm while asleep. Although he had little formal education and no medical training, this Midwestern farmer correctly diagnosed illnesses and recommended treatments for thousands of people around the world. He also time-traveled extensively and predicted many important world events that have since come to pass.

AURAS

A personal energy field known as an *aura* surrounds each of us. Sensitive individuals see this as a halo of colored light about three to twelve inches thick, like a cocoon around the physical body. (The haloes depicted around the heads of saints, angels, and religious figures in paintings are actually their auras.)

Our emotions affect our auras, which change color and shape as our moods shift. Bright, clear colors indicate positive emotions and good energy; dark, murky colors suggest discord or health problems. Some medical intuitives diagnose illnesses by examining the aura's appearance, and some holistic healers believe that disease exists in the aura before it manifests physically.

This personal energy field, also known as the *etheric* body, is integrally involved in psychic awareness and functioning. For instance, whenever we come into contact with something, we leave traces of etheric matter on it, just as we leave fingerprints on objects when we touch them. Psychics read information from jewelry or clothing by sensing these etheric traces.

Our auras are also extremely sensitive to what's going on in both our physical and nonphysical environments. Like personal radar, the aura picks up the subtle vibrations given off by people, animals, weather patterns, plants, the heavenly bodies, and many other forces all around us. This is how dowsers sense the presence of water and why we sometimes know how other people feel even if they don't outwardly express emotion.

It's usually easier to see a person's aura if he or she stands in front of a dark background. To see your own aura, hold your hand a few inches above a piece of dark cloth. Move your hand slowly, if necessary. Can you distinguish a faint glow extending from your fingertips?

Even if you can't see your aura, you can probably feel it. Here's an experiment you can try. Close your eyes while a friend slowly reaches for your head. Can you sense your friend's hand before it actually touches you? The highly responsive aura lets most of us know when something enters our personal space.

Once you become more aware of your aura, you can begin to both increase its capacity to sense what's going on around you and expand its range of perception. This will improve your ability to "read" other people and your environment.

THE SIXTH SENSE

Psychic activity can occur when you are awake, asleep, or in between. Everyone experiences it differently. Some people have visions, some hear sounds or voices. Others feel distinct bodily sensations such as chills, twitches, or a tingling in the spine. Many just *know* something without understanding how they know it. At times, psychic awareness expresses itself as a vague impression or gentle urge, while at other times it might demand your attention with the insistent force of a police siren.

Psychic experiences fall into several categories. *Clairvoyance* (literally, "clear seeing") is the ability to see things beyond the range of ordinary physical perception, including events that have not yet happened. Psychic visions often come to us in dreams, but they can also appear in a shiny surface—a crystal ball, a pool of water, even the hood of a well-waxed automobile. Sometimes visions of entire scenes from unbidden, or nonphysical beings— saints, angels, fairies, ghosts, elementals—seem to emerge out of nowhere, right before the eyes of the startled beholder.

A vision the painter Marc Chagall had when he was a young man inspired him to paint angels. Poverty-stricken and doubtful of his artistic calling, Chagall one night saw a huge, brilliant blue angel on the ceiling of his room. The angel, he believed, had come to give him the encouragement and confidence he needed to continue with his work.

Clairaudience is the power to hear things that don't activate our ordinary auditory mechanisms. This includes sounds too distant to be picked up by the physical ear, such as a child's cries of distress heard from miles away. Hearing things that have no physical source also falls into this category.

A few years ago, during a very difficult period in my life, I was walking alone in a state park near my home when I distinctly heard a voice say, "Go see Leslie." I looked around, but saw no one else in the vicinity, so I continued on my way and didn't give the matter much thought. Soon, the disembodied voice again ordered, "Go see Leslie," this time more firmly. After the third command, I walked to the studio of a jeweler named Leslie Wind, whom I'd met briefly on a few occasions. We immediately became fast friends, and she helped me through the challenges I was facing at the time.

Clairsentience, or "clear sensing," is the term used for those inexplicable feelings we get when we know something without having seen, heard, smelled, tasted, or touched it. Churchill's "feeling" that he and his guests should go to the bomb shelter is a good example of clairsentience. Sometimes clairsentience is accompanied by a physical sensation, such as a tingling, prickling, burning, or chill, but the actual awareness arrives via a "sixth sense," not through one of our five physical senses.

Precognition or premonition about the future, telepathy or mind reading, communication with entities in other planes of existence (also known as mediumship or channeling), psychic healing, intuitive medical diagnosis, psychokinesis (moving an object with your mind), psychometry (sensing an object's psychic vibrations), near-death experiences, and past-life recall all fall under the "psychic" heading.

These forms of enhanced awareness are often referred to as *extrasensory perception,* or ESP. However, this implies that psychic ability is something "extra," when in truth it is as common as the senses of hearing, sight, and taste.

CH

2

IT'S ALL IN YOUR MIND

The mind is like an iceberg—only the tip is revealed. Scientists acknowledge that we use only a fraction of the brain in daily life, so what's the rest doing? Although nobody knows the answer to that question, one thing is certain: We have far more potential than we utilize.

THE TWO SIDES OF THE BRAIN

The brain is divided into two hemispheres, the left and right. Psychic activity is associated with the right side of the brain—the part that's linked with creativity and visual imagery. The left brain governs our everyday, analytical thought processes and language skills. Simply stated, intuition arises from the right hemisphere, intellect from the left. The temporal lobe, which deals with both visual and auditory functioning as well as memory formation and emotional expression, also plays a role in psychic processes.

A collection of nerve fibers called the *corpus callosum* connects the two sides of the brain and allows them to communicate with each other. Generally speaking, the connection between the hemispheres is better developed in women's brains than in men's, enabling women to shift more freely between hemispheres. That's why women tend to be more in touch with their intuition than men are (hence the term *woman's intuition*). However, each of us, male or female, can improve communication between the two sides of the brain and expand our psychic capabilities.

Western society is left-brain dominated. We emphasize intellect, facts, logic, and linear thinking over intuition and imagination. As a result, most of us have been encouraged to use our intellect and to ignore or mistrust our intuition.

But why settle for only half a brain? You can strengthen your right brain by exercising it with activities such as listening to music, painting, and using your imagination. Because the right brain controls the left side of the body, natural right-handers may also be able to improve right-brain function by placing more emphasis on the left side. Use your computer's mouse with your left hand, for example, or hold the telephone receiver to your left ear.

MEDITATION

Silence is extremely rare in our noisy, fast-paced modern world. Not only are we bombarded with the omnipresent cacophony of traffic and other ambient sounds, we also clutter our immediate surroundings with TVs, radios, video games, and all sorts of busyness that may drown out the gentle voice of intuition. Although psychic insights can come to us in the stands at a football game or in the midst of a crowded shopping mall, we're generally more receptive when our minds are calm and quiet.

Meditation is one of the best ways to increase your capacity for psychic functioning. There are many types of meditation—some involve chanting or listening to music, others emphasize breathing techniques, and a few even include physical movement. All forms have a common objective, however: to still the mind and increase awareness.

In the most common approach, you sit still in a quiet place for a period of time—usually ten or more minutes—and attempt to empty your mind. You stop thinking about work, relationships, finances, and daily chores, and become fully present in the moment. Mental chatter temporarily ceases and you experience a profound state of relaxation in both mind and body. Of course, this is easier said than done and, like everything else, requires practice to perfect.

In one form of meditation known as *creative visualization*, the meditator forms a mental picture that conveys relaxation, such as waves breaking gently on the sand. *Contemplation* involves focusing on a particular object, idea, or image in order to gain greater insight into it. *Active meditation* sounds like an oxymoron, but that's what you're doing when you rake a Zen garden, walk a labyrinth, or stroll peacefully through the woods. The key is to move slowly, mindfully, remaining attentive to your motions.

The changes experienced during meditation aren't just subjective, they can be measured physically. Brain-wave frequencies decrease from the usual thirteen to thirty cycles per second to eight to thirteen cps. Heart rate and respiration also slow. And the brain steps up production of endorphins, the proteins that enhance positive feelings.

When you're in this serene state, known as the *alpha state*, it's easier to pick up the signals of your inner knowing. Your intuition receptors are more sensitive to psychic communication from other people, too. Over time, meditation also will improve your mental clarity, enabling you to focus your full attention on an idea or image without succumbing to distraction and to psychically project that image or idea to someone else.

DREAMS

Since ancient times, dreams have fascinated and mystified us. Where do they come from? Why do they happen? And most of all, what are they trying to tell us?

We all dream every night, even if we don't remember our dreams. Most people have between three and five dreams per night. Dreams provide a portal through which we can journey to other levels of awareness, including the psychic realm. By examining our dreams, we can uncover the secrets hidden in our unconscious minds. Dreams also connect us with the collective unconscious and with the myths, experiences, and archetypes that influence us individually as well as culturally.

The symbols and scenarios we encounter in our dreams give us clues that can help us solve the problems we face in our waking lives. Elias Howe, the developer of the lock-stitch sewing machine, got the idea for his invention from a dream. For ten years he'd been struggling to get his machine to work correctly. Then one night, he dreamed that a tribe of cannibals planned to eat him if he didn't figure out his conundrum. Howe looked at the cannibals' spears and noticed that there were holes in the pointed ends. This gave him the breakthrough idea he'd been searching for; he placed a hole in the tip of his sewing machine needle, and it then worked.

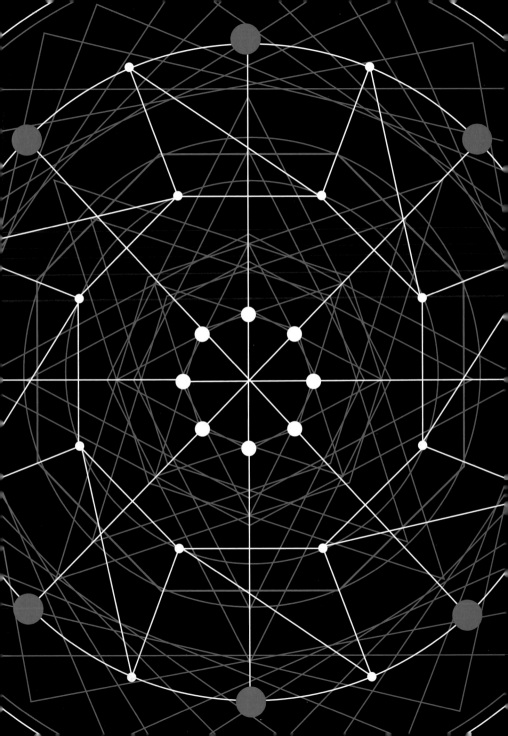

In addition to giving us insight into ourselves, our dreams plug us in to the "cosmic web" I mentioned earlier. Much like online links connecting Web sites, dreams link us to people, experiences, and information imprinted in this energetic network. Through dreams, we are sometimes able to communicate with other people—even those who may not be in the physical realm. While sleeping, Edgar Cayce psychically retrieved the knowledge of healers and physicians who'd lived long ago and used this information to help his clients. Apparently, the wisdom of the ages remains stored in a "cosmic library" even after the healers have passed on.

Shortly before my father was killed in a car accident, I dreamed that an elderly woman invited me into her home and told me of his death. After the accident, I described the woman and her home to my brother. He recognized her instantly as one of my father's friends—a friend I'd never met who had died several years earlier.

Dreams such as this enable us to transcend the boundaries of time and space to peek into the future. Seers often report that their dreams convey information about upcoming events, and we find many examples of dream prophecy in spiritual texts. In fact, precognitive dreams aren't particularly rare; lots of us have them, yet we may be baffled or unnerved by their appearance. How can we know about things that haven't happened yet?

Physicist Albert Einstein's work showed that time isn't linear. Rather than being like an expressway from the past to the future, time more closely resembles a winding mountain road. Along its course, time bends and occasionally curves back on itself, so you periodically catch glimpses of territory you won't actually reach until later in your journey—hence, the experience we call déjà vu, or "already seen." Some Eastern spiritual traditions believe that the past, present, and future all exist simultaneously, and liken time to a mountain range with many peaks and valleys.

One night I dreamed that I found a black cat on the side of a road. At first I thought it was dead, but when I touched it the cat woke up. I took it to a vet, who told me the cat had distemper and suggested performing surgery immediately. The cat didn't seem particularly ill to me, so I refused to let him operate.

The next day, as I walked home from the movies, I spotted a black cat lying in the gutter. It appeared to be paralyzed and I thought a car had hit it, although I saw no sign of injury and it didn't seem to be in pain. I knocked on the doors of all the houses in the area, but no one answered, so I took the cat to a vet. The vet surmised that the cat was near death and recommended doing an autopsy after it died to see if it had a contagious disease. Remembering my dream, I refused and took the cat home instead. Later, I returned to the neighborhood where I'd found the cat and again knocked on doors until I located its confused owner. She told me she had no idea how the cat had gotten out—it had been paralyzed from birth because its mother had contracted distemper during pregnancy. When I related my dream, she grew even more amazed and explained that the previous night, she'd dreamed her cat had disappeared.

Dreams provide a readily available, free way to expand your psychic ability. If you have trouble remembering your dreams, try keeping a dream journal. As soon as you wake up, note in it whatever details you can recollect. Gradually, as you pay closer attention to your dreams, you'll develop better recall.

TIPS FOR UNDERSTANDING YOUR DREAMS

• Dreams that recur frequently are particularly important. They are signals that your subconscious (or something else) is trying to communicate with you.

• Watch for recurring symbols and themes. Some dream symbols, such as houses, cars, water, school, and death, are common to most of us. (In Part Two, I explain the meanings of some of these familiar symbols.) But everyone has a unique set of personal symbols in addition to these.

• The mood of a dream and the feelings you experience in connection with it are clues to the dream's relevance.

• Dreams that seem "real," as opposed to those that depict things that couldn't actually happen, may predict something in the future.

MEANINGFUL COINCIDENCES

In earlier times, prophets, priests, and seers watched for omens to guide them. Such things as the movements of the heavenly bodies, the patterns formed by stones cast on a piece of cloth, and the appearance of certain animals and birds were considered portents. The Apache Indians interpreted muscle spasms in different parts of the body as signals of pending good or evil. The ancient Chinese applied a hot iron to a piece of turtle shell, causing its surface to crack in an irregular design, and then studied the cracks for meaning. In Iran and parts of northern Africa, prognosticators examined patterns in sand to determine whether happiness or misfortune was on the way.

Abundant spiritual texts and literature refer to "signs." In *Richard II*, Shakespeare wrote:

> The bay trees in our country are all withered,
>
> And meteors fright the fixed stars of heaven,
>
> The pale-faced moon looks bloody on the earth,
>
> And lean-looked prophets whisper fearful change...
>
> These signs forerun the death or fall of kings.

Many common sayings and accepted ideas involve signs. For example, a black cat crossing the street is often considered a harbinger of bad luck (although black cats are fortunate symbols for me, representing creativity and freedom). The sailors' rhyme, "Red sky at night, sailors' delight; red sky in the morning, sailors take warning," describes signs that served as guides to early navigators.

Even those of us who like to consider ourselves "rational" accept the validity of certain signs. We may even connect them with meanings or outcomes. For instance, a rainbow is a common symbol of good luck. This connection comes from the fact that a rainbow is produced by the sun's rays shining through droplets of water, so it tells us that the rain will soon end. We accept meteorological signs, such as wind patterns and changes in barometric pressure, as harbingers of weather conditions. But why are these indicators any more trustworthy than dream images or the appearance of certain animals? We acknowledge the validity of atmospheric signs because over time, they have proved to be accurate with a reasonable degree of consistency. If you pay attention to other signs, you'll discover the same is true of them.

Whenever I find coins on the street or in other unexpected places, I know I'll soon receive money. This sign has proven valid hundreds of times over the years, and I know it to be accurate. Signs may also manifest as physical sensations. Burning ears, for example, are said to indicate that someone is talking about you. Meaningful coincidences such as these are signals alerting us to pay attention, take a particular action, or prepare for something that's about to happen.

Signs are as unique as the individuals for whom they are intended; in other words, your inner wisdom might not speak to you in the same way that mine speaks to me. But if you stay alert, you'll probably start to notice that certain things occur in connection with certain other things. You may stub your toe or see a yellow car or hear a particular song when your higher consciousness is trying to get your attention. Once you learn to recognize and interpret signs, you'll better understand what's happening in the present and what the future holds for you—and be able to make the best of that knowledge.

MENTAL TELEPATHY

Recently, a man I know was getting ready to retire and felt very anxious about the prospect. As the date approached, old friends from all over the world started calling him. He hadn't talked to some of these people in quite a while, and they didn't know about his retirement, but the "vibes" he was putting out strongly urged them to check in with him.

Because we live in an energy matrix that links us psychically with everyone else on the planet, every thought, word, emotion, and deed generates vibrations that can be felt by other people in the web. Consequently, we have the potential to communicate telepathically with anyone we choose at any time, regardless of the distance between us, simply by putting our minds to it. How many times have you answered the phone to hear on the line the voice of the person you were just thinking about? This common occurrence is a good example of mental telepathy, or mind reading.

Although most telepathic communication appears to happen unintentionally or without conscious effort, this psychic ability can be honed and used purposefully. In fact, it can be a very handy skill to have when more conventional methods of communication fail. Once you get good at it, you'll find telepathy is even faster than e-mail!

Developing your mind-reading powers can also give you valuable insights into the people with whom you come into contact every day. You'll be able to sense how others are reacting to you and what they truly mean, even when they don't express it verbally. You'll know if someone is lying to you. You'll also be able to intuit if another person needs your assistance or wants your attention.

Telepathy involves both projection and perception. You use your projective ability to affect something with the force of your mind, like when you send mental messages to another person, focus healing energy on someone, or otherwise project your psychic powers outward. When you allow your mind to receive telepathic communication from someone else, pick up impressions from an inanimate object, or let your intuition guide you, you are using your perceptive skills.

Some of us are better "senders" while others are better "receivers." People who have keen powers of concentration tend to be good at projecting thoughts to others, while imaginative individuals whose minds are flexible can usually pick up impressions more readily. When trying to communicate telepathically with another person, it's best to stay relaxed and open. Don't try too hard. Don't second-guess yourself or get too analytical. The first impression that pops into your head is usually the most accurate.

You'll probably discover that you can "read" some people better than others and that some people can read you more easily than others. Twins are notoriously good at reading each other's minds. Family members, too, may be adept at communicating telepathically. My mother and I make great bridge partners because we can send mental messages back and forth, telling each other which cards to play.

TRAINING THE MIND

From the moment we emerge on this planet, our minds are programmed with ideas, information, attitudes, and beliefs. Our families, schools, society, religious institutions, and the media all play roles in molding our thought processes and our concepts about the world.

The expectations and preconceptions we hold influence what happens to us. As author Anais Nin said, "We don't see things the way they are, we see them the way we are." If we expect to experience something in a certain way, most likely that's what will occur. For instance, if you expect to have a good time at a party, you probably will. But if something differs radically from our expectations, many of us might discount its validity. That's what often happens when we have psychic experiences that don't fit in with our "logical" preconceptions.

Because the mind is so flexible and impressionable, you can train it to perceive and function in a more intuitive manner. Like your arms and legs, your "psychic muscles" grow stronger with use. Many of the techniques in Part Two are mental exercises designed to develop the intuitive regions of your mind that have grown flabby from neglect.

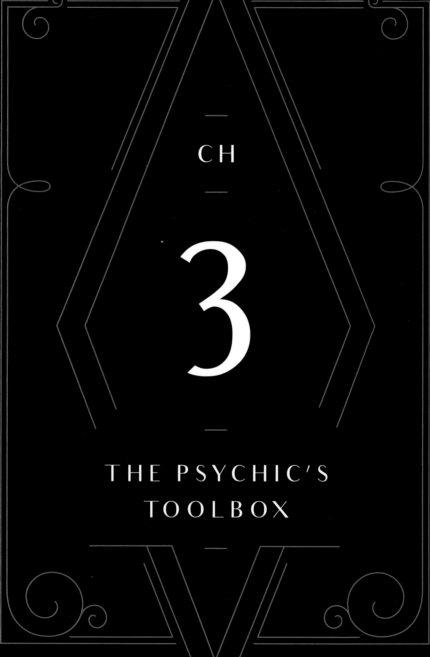

CH

3

THE PSYCHIC'S
TOOLBOX

For thousands of years, wise men and women have sought guidance from oracles such as the *I Ching*, tarot, runes, and astrology. Oracles are tools that help us tap in to our own inner guidance and connect with other realms of consciousness. They bridge the gap between the known and the unknown.

Oracles, divination tools, and metaphysical arts such as astrology and numerology expand our awareness in many ways. They enable us to gain insight into other people, see what's going on below the surface in perplexing situations, and get information about the future. Using these systems and devices also strengthens our intuitive ability.

Psychics, magicians, and metaphysicians today often employ one or more oracles in their work, just as they have for millennia. Although proficiency requires practice and in some cases study, these tools allow even a novice to crack open the doors of perception. In Part Two, I suggest a number of quick and easy techniques that will help you improve your psychic powers.

Experiment with the oracles you find intriguing. Each has its own advantages, limitations, and applications. If you're like most people, you'll find yourself drawn to certain tools and systems, and you'll probably exhibit greater facility with some than with others. If you make an effort to expand your ability, in time you'll develop a degree of expertise that can broaden your horizons in countless directions.

HOW DO ORACLES WORK?

Most divination devices operate on the premise that the answers to all questions already exist and that some part of you—your subconscious, higher mind, inner wisdom, or whatever your choose to call it—knows the answers. The trick is to access this information and bring it into your awareness. Through symbols, colors, meaningful patterns, movement, and imagery, oracles help you bypass your rational, logical intellect and its limited understanding so you can see the big picture.

Some years ago, for example, I wanted to leave my job at a furniture store. I never make an important decision without consulting an oracle, so I asked the *I Ching*, the ancient Chinese *Book of Changes*, for advice. The *I Ching* said I should wait. Before long, the company was sold and I was laid off. (Interestingly, I couldn't have known that the company would be sold because the transfer occurred as a result of an unexpected accident.) Then I was able to collect unemployment compensation while I looked for another job. Because I'd taken the oracle's advice, I ended up in a more advantageous position than I would have if I'd followed the promptings of my conscious mind alone.

Although certain oracles, including the *I Ching* and runes, have long and rich histories, anything that triggers your inner wisdom can be used as a tool for divination. Tarot cards, with their colorful images, are certainly prettier than an ordinary poker deck, but either one will work. Dozens of intriguing and imaginative oracles are now available. You can even create your own.

Divination tools serve as direct links to your intuition—they trigger insights and awarenesses you might not have received otherwise. They also are intuition builders that strengthen your psychic skills. The more you work with oracles, the sharper your extrasensory powers will become.

POPULAR DIVINATION TOOLS

Because each oracle provides information in a slightly different way, you may prefer one tool in some circumstances and another in other situations. The *I Ching*, for instance, rarely gives yes or no answers, but a pendulum is very good at responding to these types of queries. In my opinion, the tarot, because it contains seventy-eight cards, can offer more shades of meaning than the runes, which have only twenty-four letters. But the runes often give a more direct answer. Each person has his or her favorite tool, so I suggest you experiment with several to see which you like best.

The Tarot

Some researchers believe the Knights Templar brought the oracle from the Holy Land to Europe with them after the Crusades. Evidence suggests that seventy-eight-card tarot decks much like the ones we're familiar with today might have been used for telling fortunes in Italy and France during the Renaissance, and that our present-day playing cards may have evolved from these early decks.

The tarot is composed of two sections, known as the minor arcana and the major arcana (arcana means "mysterious knowledge"). Early decks may have contained only the major arcana. Typically, the minor arcana is divided into four suits (wands, pentacles, cups, and swords) and includes numbered cards from ace to ten, plus four court cards per suit. Cards in this portion of the tarot describe everyday matters. The suit of wands relates to creativity and inspiration; pentacles correspond to money and physical matters; cups deal with emotions and relationships; and swords are linked with communication and ideas. The numbers on the cards are also significant and add detail to the meanings of the suits as follows:

1 = beginnings, focused energy
2 = partnerships, cooperation
3 = development, growth
4 = solidification, stability, rigidity
5 = dispersion, instability, challenges
6 = give and take, practical application
7 = individual approaches and expression
8 = intensification of energy, establishment
9 = expansion, increase
10 = achievement, maximum development

The major arcana describes "fated" or "cosmic" conditions having implications that extend beyond personal or mundane matters. It consists of twenty-two cards having these basic meanings:

Fool = innocence, beginnings, trust
Magician = hidden powers
High Priestess = intuition, emotions

Empress = mature female, self-esteem

Emperor = mature male, organization, pragmatism

Hierophant = leadership, higher knowledge

Lovers = choices, union of opposites, relationships

Chariot = situations beyond your control, mysterious forces at work

Strength = overcoming weaknesses, inner power

Hermit = retreat, reflection, self-reliance

Wheel of Fortune = a change for the better, good luck

Justice = trial, equality, honesty, rectification

Hanged Man = relinquishing control, letting go

Death = transformation, loss and rebirth

Temperance = moderation, balance, acceptance

Devil = obsession, fear, lack of discrimination

Tower = major change, freedom, destruction of the old

Star = hope, ideals, happiness

Moon = illusion, secrets, the subconscious

Sun = clarity, contentment, self-expression

Judgment = choices, change, regeneration

Universe = progress, order and harmony, achievement

The tarot can be used to gain insight into a problem or situation, to divine the future, or as a meditation aid. In what's known as a *reading*, cards are individually drawn from a deck or laid out in special arrangements called *spreads*.

It's a good idea to keep a journal of your readings so you can learn from them and increase your interpretive ability over time. In Part Two, I give you some quick and easy techniques utilizing the tarot for developing your psychic skills.

Runes

According to Norse mythology, the god Odin brought the wisdom of the runes to humankind after a painful ordeal in which he hung upside down for nine days on the sacred world-tree Yggdrasil. Used throughout Northern Europe and Scandinavia for two millennia (until Christians banned them in 1639), these magical and shamanic tools were brought by Viking and Saxon invaders to the British Isles, where they were a common form of divination until the Industrial Revolution. In the United States, runes gained popularity during the 1960s and 1970s as a result of J. R. R. Tolkien's *The Lord of the Rings*, which introduced many readers to Teutonic mythology.

The word *rune* means "secret" or "to whisper." These ancient symbols are tools for communicating with the inner self as well as with the Divine. Each rune is a letter of an alphabet. Today, for use as an oracle, the simple glyphs can be inscribed on pieces of stone, wood, ceramic, metal, or bone, although they may also be drawn on cards or just about any other surface. In a reading, one or more runes are drawn or cast; they may also be laid out in special patterns in much the same manner as tarot cards.

Twenty-four runes make up what's known as the Elder Futhark, the old Teutonic alphabet (the most popular version of the runes). Each of these runes is named for an animal, emotion, familiar object, or deity. Ralph Blum, author of the best-selling *Book of Runes*, recently added an extra, blank rune called *Wyrd*. *Ogham* runes, based on the ancient Celtic alphabet, link each letter to a tree that the Druids considered sacred.

When used as an oracle, runes describe certain energies, with each rune offering specific information or advice. The basic meanings of the Elder Futhark of the Norse/Teutonic runes are as follows:

ᚠ *Fehu* = gain, achievement

ᚢ *Uruz* = strength, improvement, enthusiasm

ᚦ *Thurisaz* = protection, conflict, stubbornness

ᚨ *Ansuz* = advice, wisdom

ᚱ *Raidho* = travel, communication

ᚲ *Kenaz* = energy, opening up, respite

ᚷ *Gifu* or *Gebo* = a gift, love, relationships

ᚹ *Wunjo* = joy, success

ᚺ *Hagall* or *Hagalaz* = limits, delays

ᚾ *Nied* or *Naudiz* = difficulties, be patient

ᛁ *Isa* = cooling trend, frustration, obstacle

ᛃ *Jera* = rewards, successful outcome

ᛇ *Eihwaz* = overcoming hardships

ᛈ *Perdhro* = secrets, surprises, intuition

ᛉ *Eolh* = friendship, opportunity

ᛋ *Sigel* or *Sowilo* = victory, vitality

ᛏ *Tir* or *Tiwaz* = increase, health, success, passion

ᛒ *Beorc* or *Berkana* = beginnings, birth

M *Ehwaz* = gradual progress, change

M *Mannaz* = seek aid, be positive, modesty

Γ *Laguz* or *Lagaz* = intuition, ability to succeed

◊ *Ing* or *Inguz* = good fortune, renewal

M *Daeg* or *Dagaz* = slow growth, gradual change

⦉ *Othel* or *Otila* = possessions, inheritance

In Part Two, I suggest ways to use runes to gaze into the future, solve problems, and strengthen intuition.

I Ching

Believed to have been created in China by Confucius 3,000 years ago, the *I Ching*, or *Book of Changes*, is composed of sixty-four patterns known as hexagrams, each having a different meaning. In 1950, Princeton University published a translation of this ancient oracle by Richard Wilhelm and C. F. Baynes, introducing many people in the West to the *I Ching*.

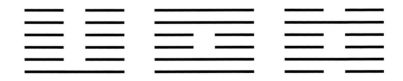

The traditional method for consulting this oracle required the querent to ask a question and then draw yarrow sticks in order to determine which of the hexagrams provided the answer to the seeker's question. Today, the most common way to get an answer is to toss three coins together six times while contemplating your question. The way the coins fall—with heads or tails up—on each toss is significant. Tails are connected with the "yin" or receptive force, heads with the "yang" or assertive force. There are sixty-four possible combinations, and each one corresponds to one of the hexagrams in the book. Your question is answered by the complete hexagram formed of six yin or yang lines; certain lines within the hexagram symbol provide further illumination, as each line has its own specific meaning.

Some new *I Ching* kits use cards, marbles, numbered sticks, or computer programs to produce answers. You can even get *I Ching* readings online. Like the tarot or runes, the *I Ching* can be used for problem solving, reflection, and meditation, or to gain insight into the future.

Pendulums

Most people associate dowsing with hunting for water that's deep in the ground, but actually, it is a broader psychic art that enables the dowser to tap into hidden energy patterns with the help of a sensing device. A pendulum is one such device. Basically a small weight on the end of a chain or string, a pendulum is held loosely and allowed to swing of its own accord in response to a question. Used in this manner, the pendulum lets you connect with your inner wisdom to gain insight into current or future matters.

Generally, a pendulum held in front of the questioner swings from side to side when the answer is "no." When the answer is "yes," the pendulum swings back and forth. A clockwise circling motion suggests that a particular situation is positive or favorable; counterclockwise movement indicates a negative or unfavorable condition. However, you can instruct or "program" your pendulum to respond according to your own code.

Pendulums may also be utilized to find lost or hidden objects, or to provide information about people, places, or things. When the late astrologer Betty Lundsted wanted to find a place to live in New York City, she used a pendulum to dowse a map of the city's streets and the numbers of specific buildings. As a result, she found an apartment that was right for her and spared herself a lot of legwork. Some pendulums are designed for treasure hunting—they come apart and can be filled or "loaded" with particular substances to aid the dowser's search for water, gold, or whatever is the quarry.

Pendulums can be made of just about anything, although dowsers generally advise against using lead because it blocks subtle energy vibrations. You can make a simple device by tying a nail, button, or other small weight to the end of a piece of string about six inches long. Pendulums made of brass or stainless steel are readily available commercially. Some people prefer pendulums weighted with semiprecious stones or quartz crystals. The most important thing is that it feels "right" in your hand.

To use a pendulum, hold the cord or chain so the weight dangles loosely above the object or area you are dowsing, then ask a question. Pretty soon, you'll feel the pendulum start to swing—try not to influence its movement. In Part Two, I offer some exercises that use the pendulum to develop your psychic ability.

Crystal Balls and Other Scrying Devices

Scrying is the art of gazing into a smooth surface to see beyond the range of your normal vision, to look into the future or gain insight into current situations. Any shiny surface will work—a crystal ball, a dark mirror, a glossy piece of metal, a pool of still water. The device itself doesn't produce the images; it merely serves as an aid to your intuition.

A genuine quartz crystal ball is a favorite tool for scrying because its complex inner structure contains lots of swirls, reflective plates, hollows, and cloudy wisps, which easily take on meaningful shapes that your "second sight" can interpret. Another reason for their popularity is that crystals are living entities, so they actually interact with whoever uses them. Over time, a crystal ball will become a close friend and helper, and it should be treated as such.

To scry, relax your mind and gaze quietly into the reflective tool you are using. A few minutes of meditation or breathing exercises beforehand can be beneficial. Try not to hold any preconceptions or force images to appear—stay open and receptive to whatever comes into your field of vision. Thoughts or feelings that arise during the process should also be considered.

If nothing much happens the first few times you attempt to scry, don't get discouraged—it could take some time and practice to master this psychic skill. In the beginning, you probably won't want to spend more than ten minutes or so gazing into your scrying tool. If you start to feel tired, distracted, or impatient, stop and come back to it another time. After you become more proficient, you may discover that visions appear to you almost instantaneously or that you can spend longer periods working with your crystal ball (or other device).

Trust your hunches and the impressions you receive. Write down your visions and experiences afterward, even if you don't understand exactly what they mean—their significance may become clearer at a later date.

INTUITIVE AND DIVINATION ARTS

For centuries, astrology, numerology, hand analysis, and graphology have been used to immediately gain insight into people. These ancient esoteric arts don't require real psychic ability, yet they enable a skilled practitioner to see into the deepest part of an individual's psyche and uncover traits or motivations that the person may not even be aware of. Astrology and numerology are also very effective tools for predicting the future. Although it takes years of study and practice to become proficient in these arts, even a little knowledge will reveal quite a bit about someone.

Astrology

Ralph Waldo Emerson explained that "Astrology is astronomy brought to Earth and applied to the affairs of men." Used throughout the world, in one form or another, for thousands of years, astrology's origins lie veiled in the mists of antiquity. Early cultures viewed the sun, moon, and planets as gods and goddesses whose awesome powers influenced everything that happened here on earth. Ancient structures such as Stonehenge and the Temple of Luxor suggest that our ancestors possessed an advanced knowledge of the skies and could predict celestial movements with great accuracy.

Today, most people think astrology is the predictions they read in the daily newspaper, but it is actually a vast, complex, and amazingly versatile scientific art. Professional astrologers use it not only to analyze personality, but also to track weather patterns, predict earth changes, solve crimes, reduce job-related injuries, diagnose illnesses, and make money in the stock market. One form of astrology known as horary also answers questions. The late Olivia Barclay, a well-known authority in this field, successfully used it to find lost pets.

When someone asks, "What's your sign?" what he or she really means is, Where was the sun positioned in the sky on the day of your birth? This single factor is probably the most significant personality indicator in your birth chart. (A birth chart, or horoscope, by the way, is a two-dimensional diagram of the heavens that shows the positions of the celestial bodies as they appeared at the time and from the place of a person's birth. Charts can also be calculated for the birth of a business, country, or event.)

In Part Two, I reveal some key traits and qualities of people born during each of the twelve sun signs to help you "unmask" the people you know. Aquarians, for example, are independent and unconventional thinkers; Cancers tend to devote themselves to their families; and Leos enjoy being the center of attention.

Astrologers also plot the positions of the moon, planets, and various other bodies when "casting" a chart. Each of these governs certain aspects of life experience, and when considered together they provide a detailed picture of an individual. (My book *Planets in Signs* describes in detail the meanings of the sun, moon, and planets in all the zodiac signs.)

The cyclic travels of the moon and planets, and the apparent movement of the sun, instigate changes in our personal lives and in the world around us. We see this most plainly in the way the moon's phases affect the tides and how the sun's position relative to the earth changes the seasons. By observing the cycles of the heavenly bodies, astrologers can predict both large-scale events and individual experiences well into the future.

Numerology

What's in a name? From the perspective of numerology, quite a lot. Like astrology, numerology (the study of numbers) is a tool for both analyzing personality and divination. And, like astrology, it combines science with art. Numerology doesn't require psychic ability—although intuition often comes into play during its application—but a knowledgeable numerologist can glean so much information about a person from simply adding together numbers that she or he may appear to be relying on a sixth sense.

Rooted in the ancient past, numerology was handed down to us from the Greek mathematician and mystic Pythagorus. Its tenets are based in the principles of the Kabbalah and esoteric Judaism, but it also has close connections to astrology and the tarot, as well as to many other metaphysical practices.

Numerologists examine both your birth date and your name to ascertain your personality, potential, life purpose, and much more. Each letter of your full name corresponds to a number, and each number represents certain qualities, as follows:

1	2	3	4	5	6	7	8	9
A	B	C	D	E	F	G	H	I
J	K	L	M	N	O	P	Q	R
S	T	U	V	W	X	Y	Z	

1 = individuality, assertiveness, beginnings, leadership

2 = union, adaptability, balance, receptivity

3 = expansion, creativity, sociability, expression

4 = stability, practicality, discipline, form

5 = change, freedom, movement, activity

6 = beauty, harmony, affection, comfort

7 = introspection, solitude, wisdom, mysticism

8 = pragmatism, business, money, recognition

9 = service, spirituality, compassion, endings

11 = humanitarianism, ideals, innovation, community

22 = power, authority, knowledge, success

After assigning a number to each letter, add them together. The total will most likely be a double-digit number, in which case you add the digits in the total together until you've "reduced" it to a single-digit number. (Note: eleven and twenty-two are usually left unreduced.) The sum of the numbers that correspond to the vowels in your name shows your inner nature or private side. The sum of the consonants' values describes your outer personality and how other people see you. The total of both reveals your destiny, or life path.

In addition to your name, you'll want to consider your birth date, which tells what lessons you are learning in this lifetime. Add the number of the month of your birth to the date, then add the four digits in the year, and reduce the sum until you get a single digit.

With each year, you begin a different cycle. To predict what's likely to happen during these cycles, add your birth month and date to the year, then reduce the total to a single digit. The numerological tenor of the times is similar to the number interpretations given above. If the reduced number of the cycle you are in this year is one, for instance, this is a period for new beginnings and asserting your individuality. If you're in a four cycle, you'll feel more like securing your position and devoting yourself to practical matters.

Hand Analysis

Sometimes called palmistry, hand analysis is really the study of the entire hand—the back and fingers as well as the palm—in order to deduce a person's character, strengths and weaknesses, proclivities, life experiences, health, and much more. A hand reader examines everything about the hand, including its shape, the color and texture of the skin, the fingers and fingernails, the mounds and hollows in the palm, the lines, even the many little marks (dots, slashes, stars, chains, and so on) on the palm. Our hands so accurately describe us that a hand reader who knows what to look for appears to tune in to us psychically, although it's not necessary to use ESP to analyze a hand.

In essence, your hand is a map of your life. Each part of the hand is associated with a different facet of your nature. For instance, the pinkie finger relates to your communication skills. The fleshy part of the palm opposite the thumb, called the Mound of the Moon, describes your emotions and intuition. The middle line that stretches across your palm reveals your mental powers.

Although you may not be able to judge a book by its cover, you can tell a great deal about a person by the appearance of his or her hand. For example, a hand that's slender and graceful with long, thin fingers suggests that the person is sensitive, intuitive, artistic, more interested in ideas than the physical world. A square, sturdy-looking hand with rather thick, blunt fingers indicates that the person is practical, handy, a "doer." Flexible fingers show adaptability; stiff fingers reveal tenacity. A simple, straightforward

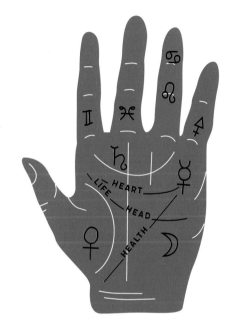

person will have a palm with few lines, while a complex, highly intelligent individual's palm will be crisscrossed with numerous lines.

Sometimes you encounter a person whose hands seem as though they should belong to someone else, they are so incongruous with the rest of the person's body. In such cases, the face shows the outer person—the image presented to the world—while the hands reveal the inner nature. A publisher I know appears quite fragile—she's petite and small-boned, with a milky-white, porcelainlike complexion. Her hands, though, are on the large side, with strong fingers and somewhat coarse, thick skin that's noticeably darker than that on her face. This successful businesswoman is often underestimated because people think she is demure and delicate; however, any palm reader would immediately spot the tough, dynamic qualities she possesses.

The hand you don't normally use (the left, if you are right-handed) shows the abilities and tendencies you were born with—and some say your past lives. The dominant hand indicates how you've utilized your birth qualities. Important life events and experiences, both physical and emotional, leave their marks on your hand. An injury might show up as a dot on the head line; a divorce could cause a break in the heart line. By examining these and many other details, a hand reader can see what's transpired in your past and, to a lesser degree, what's likely to occur in your future.

Part Two contains a number of tips that will help you to immediately size up the people you meet, simply by looking at their hands.

Graphology

Each of us writes in a unique and distinctive manner, and our handwriting reveals a great deal about us. How we dot our i's and cross our t's—as well as how we slant our letters, form loops, and position lines on a page—describe our temperaments, intellectual capacity, vocational potential, health, relationship needs, and much more.

The use of graphology, or handwriting analysis, to judge personality dates back at least two millennia. An early Roman historian is said to have looked at Julius Caesar's handwriting and determined from the spacing between the emperor's letters that he was mean-spirited. Graphology rose to popularity in Europe during the eighteenth and nineteenth centuries and, before long, many noted men and women in both the sciences and arts—including Johann Wolfgang von Goethe, Charles Dickens, George Sand, and Albert Einstein—learned the skill of handwriting analysis. Today, graphologists help police solve crimes, evaluate job applicants' aptitudes for prospective employers, and assist psychologists in assessing personality.

Like the other fields of study we've discussed, graphology doesn't actually require psychic ability, though intuition often enters into the interpretive process. However, a knowledgeable graphologist may seem psychic because he or she can accurately read a person from a few lines of handwritten text. With just a little understanding of this ancient art, you'll be able to spot key ingredients in an individual's character, too.

Writing is largely an unconscious process, and the formation of letters is governed mainly by the right brain—although language itself is primarily a left-brain function. To some extent, however, we can consciously choose to write in a certain way if we wish, in order to enhance or diminish particular qualities in our natures. In Part Two, I suggest a number of ways to use handwriting for problem solving and personal growth. For example, increasing the amount of space you leave between words can improve your intuition.

PART
TWO

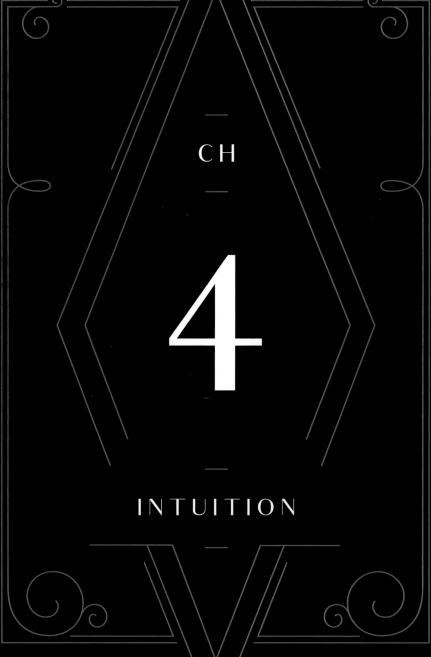

CH

4

INTUITION

One rainy afternoon, I was driving down the interstate when I suddenly felt myself being drawn toward an exit I hadn't planned to take. I didn't understand why it seemed important that I turn off the highway, but I've learned to trust my hunches, so I took the exit. As I drove up the ramp and my elevation increased, I could see further down the interstate. Up ahead, a truck had skidded on the wet pavement and its trailer lay overturned on the road, blocking traffic.

Although my physical vision was limited, my "second sight" had witnessed the accident and warned me in time to avoid the jam that resulted. While other vehicles sat motionless on the highway, I zipped around the tie-up and found an alternate route to my destination.

Undoubtedly, you've had similar experiences. We usually consider these "hunches" to be inexplicable, isolated incidents. But once you begin paying attention to them, you'll notice that they actually occur rather frequently. Where do these impressions come from? Why do they happen? And how can we benefit from them?

Intuition comes from the Latin word *intueri*, which means to look within. It is the ability to perceive, know, or feel things beyond the range of the conscious mind. In her book *Awakening Intuition*, Mona Lisa Schulz, M.D., Ph.D., describes intuition as "an internal form of perception of things that are not directly in front of us in the world."

As I stated before, everyone possesses intuition. Intuitive impulses may come as thoughts, visions, sounds, body sensations, or emotions—each of us experiences intuition differently. Practicing the simple techniques in this chapter on a regular basis will help you strengthen your intuitive powers. You don't have to do all of them—experiment, then choose the ones that work best for you. Most of these exercises can be performed in ten minutes or less, but don't expect immediate results. Intuition is like any other ability—the more you use it, the sharper it will become.

Turn off the TV.

Noise and distractions can drown out the voice of your intuition. Turn off the television and just sit quietly for a certain period during every day—and don't leave the TV on in the background when you aren't watching it.

Guess who is on the phone before you answer it.

We've all had the experience of getting a phone call or letter from someone we'd just been thinking about—that's because our thoughts actually flow out toward other people and touch them on an intuitive level. The next time the phone rings, try to guess who's calling before you look at the caller ID.

Sense colors.
Take five sheets of colored paper in different hues, close your eyes, and mix them up. Lay the sheets of paper out on a table. With your eyes still closed, hold your hand over each sheet and see if you can feel what color it is.

Flip a coin and try to guess how it will fall.
Often used for decision making, flipping a coin can also be a good exercise for developing your intuitive ability. Keep track of your "hits" and "misses."

Influence a coin toss.
Flip a coin and while it's in the air, try to affect which way it will fall. Visualize the coin landing in the heads-up position. Concentrate and project this "directive" to the coin. How many times are you successful?

Sense pictures in envelopes.
Cut pictures of the four elements from magazines—one of the sky to represent air, one showing a body of water, one depicting fire, and one of a landscape to symbolize earth. Place each picture in an envelope, then mix up the envelopes. Can you intuit which envelope contains which element?

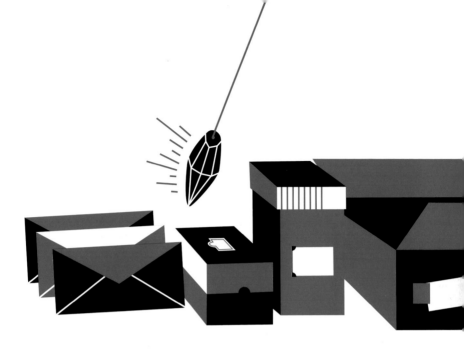

Sense objects concealed in closed boxes.

Place five objects of different shapes and colors—for instance, a comb, a shell, a spool of thread, a lighter, and a pen—inside five identical boxes. Close the boxes and then shuffle them around (or ask someone else to shuffle them) so you don't know which item is in which box. Then hold your hand over each box and try to sense what's inside.

Use a pendulum to "dowse" concealed objects.

You can use a pendulum to determine what's hidden in a box or envelope. Hold the pendulum about six inches above the container and ask, for example, "Is the shell in this box?" The pendulum will begin to swing of its own accord to answer "yes" or "no." (For more about pendulums, see Chapter 3.)

Sense which object is missing.

Ask a friend to put all but one of the objects from the previous exercise in a box together. Hold your hand over the box. Can you sense which object is missing?

Use a pendulum to sense what's missing.

Hold the pendulum about 6 inches (15 cm) above the container and ask, "Is the shell [or whatever] in this box?" If the pendulum swings back and forth, signifying "yes," inquire about another object until you get a "no" response. Were you correct?

Imagine a circle of dark blue between your eyebrows.

This spot is considered to be the site of your "third eye." Dark blue is the color of the psychic realm. By closing your eyes and focusing your attention on this energy center or "chakra" (as it is called in Sanskrit), you increase its power and receptivity.

Imagine a yellow circle in the area of your solar plexus.

This spot between your chest and navel is linked with your emotions, which play a part in intuition. By focusing your attention on this chakra, you increase your ability to tune in to other people's emotions.

Awaken your chakras.

There are seven major chakras in your body, running up from the base of the spine to the top of your head. When you awaken these energy centers, you improve your psychic sensing ability as well as your overall physical and emotional health. During meditation, focus your attention on each one individually, beginning with the "root" chakra at the base of your spine. The second chakra is located a few inches below your navel. The third is at your solar plexus. The fourth is near your heart, and the fifth is at the bottom of your neck, between your collarbones. The sixth chakra is between your eyebrows, and the seventh is at the crown of your head.

Consult a crystal ball.

A crystal ball is an excellent "scrying" tool—when you gaze into its multidimensional center, you can see all sorts of images. Relax your mind and allow your intuition to pick up impressions. Note what you feel and sense, as well as what you see. What do these perceptions mean to you? (Tip: Genuine quartz crystal balls are better than Austrian crystal or glass, but they're also more expensive.)

Gaze at the smooth surface of a calm pool of water.

This scrying technique is similar to gazing into a crystal ball. Relax your mind and let your eyes perceive whatever impressions or visions appear on the shiny surface of the water. Allow your imagination to pick out shapes, pictures, and patterns. Do these images have any special meaning for you?

Meditate.

Sit quietly, with your eyes closed, for at least ten minutes every day. Try to still your mind and remain calm and receptive. Focus on your breathing, paying complete attention to each inhalation and exhalation. If thoughts pop into your head, gently release them and bring your attention back to your breathing. In time, you will experience fewer mental interruptions and achieve a deeper state of relaxation.

Program your inner clock.

Once you master this psychic skill, you'll never need an alarm clock. Before going to sleep at night, instruct your subconscious mind to wake you at a particular time. Visualize the face of a clock showing the wake-up time. Soon, you'll be able to awaken just before your alarm goes off.

Listen with your left ear.

The left side of your body is connected with the right side of the brain— the hemisphere that governs intuition. When you talk on the phone, hold the receiver to your left ear to strengthen your right brain.

Use your computer mouse with your left hand.

Like the previous technique, this one strengthens your right brain and your intuition by working the left hand.

Write with your left hand.

If you are right-handed, try writing with your left hand for a few minutes each day. Don't worry about neatness or legibility. The point is to strengthen your right brain and your intuition by focusing attention on your left hand.

Draw with your left hand.

Right-handers, don't try to draw a recognizable image, simply relax and let your hand move freely, guided by your intuition, creating lines, shapes, and patterns. The effort of using your left hand strengthens your right brain and intuition, while the act of "automatic drawing" triggers responses from your subconscious.

Interpret your drawing.

When you've finished the previous exercise, take a few minutes to study your drawing. What do you see in it? Do any of the shapes and patterns you drew have special meaning for you?

Improve your tactile sensitivity.

This exercise strengthens your intuition by enhancing your tactile sensitivity. Select three natural fabrics that have rich and distinctly different textures—silk, velvet, and wool, for example. Close your eyes and spend a few moments stroking each fabric with your left hand. As you touch each piece of material, allow your fingertips to fully experience the sensations that arise, and send these impressions to your right brain.

Sense fabrics psychically.

This exercise is an extension of the previous one. After you have familiarized yourself with the textures of different fabrics, "feel" them without physically touching them. Close your eyes, hold your hand a few inches above each piece of fabric, and "stroke" it—can you determine which is which?

Sense other materials psychically.

It may be easier for you to sense the vibrations in substances that are very different in character. Try to identify iron, wood, stone, plastic, and glass by holding your hand a few inches above each material to sense its energetic composition.

Keep a dream journal.

We receive information from both our subconscious and the divine realms in our dreams. To improve dream recall and better understand your dreams, write them down in a journal upon awakening each morning. (For more about dreams, see Chapter 1.)

Keep a notepad on your bedside table to record dreams.

If you wake up in the middle of the night, jot down a few quick notes about what you were dreaming—if you wait until morning, you may not remember clearly.

Carry index cards to record insights.

Intuitive insights can come to you at any time, often when you aren't expecting them. Carry a few index cards in your pocket or purse so you can jot down these impressions when they arise.

Feel your aura, exercise 1.

Hold your hands up in front of you, a few inches apart, with the palms facing each other. Can you feel the energy emanating from them? Try holding your palms about a foot apart, then slowly move them closer together until you can feel your aura. (For more about auras, see Chapter 1.)

Feel your aura, exercise 2.

Hold your hand with the palm down, a couple of inches above your opposite arm. Run your hand slowly along your arm without actually touching it. Can you feel your aura? Do the same thing with your leg. Can you feel your aura there, too?

See the aura around your hand.

Hold your hand over a piece of dark cloth. Relax and gaze at your hand, without trying to focus too sharply on it. Can you see a soft halo around your hand or extending from your fingertips? That's your aura, or etheric body. (Tip: It may help to move your hand around a little or gaze just off to the side of your hand, rather than looking directly at it.)

See a pet's aura.

Animals have auras, too. See if you can detect a faint halo of light around your pet's body.

See a plant's aura.

Like other living things, plants have auras. Try to see the aura around a tree, shrub, or houseplant. If you can't see it, you may be able to feel it if you hold your hand an inch or two away from the plant.

See a crystal's aura.

Quartz crystals are living entities, so they have auras, too. Relax and gaze at a favorite crystal. Can you distinguish a faint halo glowing around the crystal? (Note: This will happen only with natural quartz crystals—leaded crystals aren't alive.)

Make a crystal shine brighter.

Crystals respond to our attention. You can increase a quartz crystal's brilliance by focusing on it and sending it loving thoughts. If you wish, you can rub it gently or talk to it. Notice how the crystal begins to shine more brightly as you give it attention.

Focus on whatever you are doing.

This sounds simpler than it is. Most of the time, we try to do several things simultaneously and allow our minds to wander. By concentrating completely on the task at hand—even seemingly mindless chores such as folding laundry or washing dishes—you train yourself to ignore distractions and strengthen your focusing skills.

Press the tips of your index fingers and thumbs together.

Perhaps you've seen people do this while meditating. That's because there are nerve endings and acupressure points in the tips of your fingers that can help you relax. Gently press these together when you want to calm down or spark intuition, insights, creativity, or memories.

Press the spot between your eyebrows.

The acupressure point located on your forehead between your eyebrows is the site of the "third eye" and your psychic sight. Close your eyes and press it gently for thirty seconds to stimulate intuition.

Press the spot between your nose and upper lip.

This acupressure point is linked to concentration and memory. Close your eyes and press it gently for thirty seconds to improve mental clarity and receptivity.

Massage the Mound of the Moon on your palm.

The fleshy part at the outer, bottom part of your palm, opposite your thumb, is known as the Mound of the Moon, and it's linked with psychic ability. Gently massage this mound to stimulate your intuition.

Look at cloud formations.

As they drift through the sky, clouds constantly change shape. Lie on your back and gaze up at the sky. Relax your mind and watch the cloud formations—what images do you see in them? What impressions do they inspire in you?

Look into a flame.

Like the previous technique, this one quiets your rational mind so your intuition and inner sight can come to the fore. Sit in front of a fire or gaze into a candle's flame. Allow impressions, insights, visions, and feelings to arise in your consciousness. What do you see in the flame?

Make a flame flicker.

Light a candle and place it where it will not be affected by a breeze or draft. Focus all your attention on the flame and try to influence its movement. Can you use the power of your mind to make it flicker?

Ripple the surface of water.

Fill a shallow bowl or saucer with water and set it on a table. Sit quietly and stare at the surface of the water. Focus all of your attention on your objective as you try to create a slight ripple in the water, using only your mind to cause the movement.

Sniff peppermint essential oil.

The scent of mint heightens mental clarity. Put a drop of pure essential oil of peppermint on your wrist and sniff it to open your psychic receptors.

Sniff lavender essential oil.

Lavender promotes both mental clarity and a sense of calm. Therefore, sniffing this scent helps to enhance psychic awareness.

Focus on the *I Ching* hexagram *K'un*.

Draw the hexagram above on a piece of paper, then gaze at it for a few moments each day. *K'un* is the symbol for receptivity, and it can help you open your mind to psychic communication.

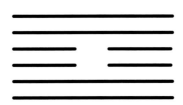

Contemplate the *I Ching* hexagram *Chung Fu*.

Chung Fu, which means "inner truth," helps you connect with your inner wisdom. Draw the hexagram above on a piece of paper, then gaze at it for a few moments each day to strengthen your intuition.

Talk to your plants.

Studies have shown that plants respond to our thoughts and words. You can strengthen your psychic powers by mentally communicating with house and garden plants—you can also influence their growth by thinking positive thoughts or sending them loving vibes.

Practice psychic communication with pets.

Animals communicate psychically with each other. They are also very sensitive to your thoughts and feelings. Relax, close your eyes, and mentally call your pet's name. Imagine your pet coming to you. With a little practice, you'll develop your projective powers and learn to communicate with your animal companion in this way.

Listen to birds.

The great Austrian mystic, Rudolf Steiner, recommended listening intently to the songs of birds as a way to increase your powers of perception. Pay attention not only to the tune, but also to the emotional quality of a bird's song. Can you sense what he or she is saying? This technique will also help you intuit what people are thinking and feeling.

Observe flowers.

Steiner also believed we could enhance our psychic powers by closely observing flowers. Relax your mind and gaze intently at a flower for a minute or two, noting small details in an objective way. Notice any feelings or impressions that arise during the process. This technique increases your sensitivity to your surroundings, enabling you to become more perceptive and receptive.

Drum to stimulate intuition.

Rhythmic sounds, such as drumming or chanting, slow brain-wave function. They often are used to induce a trance state in which your receptivity and intuition are increased. Drum yourself, or listen to a tape of rhythmic drumming to heighten your awareness before you attempt telepathy or another form of psychic activity.

Recite a mantra.

Mantras are words chosen for their particular sound quality. Repeating a mantra aloud for a period of time promotes a state of calm awareness, much like rhythmic drumming does. Often a mantra is a foreign word with which you have no other association—the sound is all that matters. If you prefer, choose a word that describes your intention, such as relax, open, or intuit.

Look at an abstract image.

In the 1920s, the Swiss psychiatrist Hermann Rorschach developed a procedure using inkblots to stimulate imagination and associative thinking. Abstract images such as inkblots or even nonrepresentational art can trigger intuition. Relax and gaze at an abstract shape—what impressions does it stir in you?

Create your own abstract image.

Dip a string in paint or ink, then slap it on a piece of paper until you sense that the image is complete. Gaze at it for a few moments. What does it say to you?

Notice recurring incidents.

Your subconscious and the higher realms are continually sending you messages. One way they do this is through creating small incidents—and major ones, if necessary—to get your attention. Be alert to symbolic incidents or patterns—do they have any deeper meanings or connections? When one of these occurs, notice what you are thinking about or doing. (See Chapter 2 for more about this.)

Pay attention to coincidences.

The Swiss psychiatrist C. G. Jung used the term "synchronicity" to describe what we usually call coincidence. As when you hear from a person you were just thinking about, so-called coincidences often indicate an intuitive contact or other psychic occurrence. Pay attention to what appear to be coincidences in your life—they could have deeper significances.

Change your handwriting.

When you write, increase the amount of space between the words in your sentences to improve your intuition. Wide spaces indicate openness and receptivity. (For more about handwriting, see Chapter 3.)

Wear amethyst jewelry.

Amethysts are connected with intuition. Wearing amethyst jewelry or carrying a piece of amethyst in your pocket can help enhance your psychic ability.

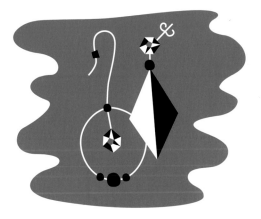

Wear opals.

Opals are also good stones for enhancing intuition. Strengthen your psychic ability by wearing opal jewelry or carrying an opal in your pocket.

Wear silver jewelry.

Silver is considered the moon's metal, and intuition is within the moon's domain. Wearing silver jewelry helps attune you to the moon's energy and your own inner voice.

Sleep with an amethyst under your pillow.

To stimulate dreams and improve dream recall, place a piece of amethyst under your pillow at night.

Play the stock market.

You don't actually have to buy any stock, just choose one or two "on a hunch" and follow their progress over a period of time. Does your hunch pay off?

Watch a horse race on TV.

Watch the Kentucky Derby or another big horse race on TV. When the horses come out on the track and enter the starting gate, try to guess which one will win. You don't have to place a bet, just see if your hunch was correct.

Pick the fastest lane in the supermarket.

Once you master this intuitive skill, you'll reduce the amount of time you waste standing in checkout lanes. When you are in a crowded store, let your intuition rather than your logic choose which lane will move most quickly.

Take advantage of the time of day.

You may find that your intuition is keener at certain times of the day or night. Note the time when you receive psychic impulses. Do they tend to occur in the morning, afternoon, evening, or late at night? If you can discern a pattern, allow yourself to "open up" to intuitive impressions at those times.

Play word association with yourself.

Open a book and close your eyes. Randomly choose a word by putting your finger down on the page. For the next five minutes, write down everything that springs to mind in connection with the word you selected, no matter how nonsensical it seems. Don't censor yourself. What does this exercise help you discover about yourself? What thoughts does it prompt?

Listen to soothing music.

Calm, relaxing, instrumental music—especially music that does not have a catchy melody—helps quiet the mind and make you more receptive to psychic impulses.

Distinguish instruments in a piece of music.

This exercise helps strengthen your attention and awareness, which are important in developing psychic ability. Pay attention to one instrument at a time when listening to instrumental music. Shift your attention from instrument to instrument, isolating its voice from the others.

Display the rune *Lagaz*.

This rune can also help you develop your intuition. Draw the rune above on a piece of paper and display it in a place where you will see it often. Gaze at it for a few minutes each day, focusing your complete attention on the symbol. (Note: Because *Lagaz* is considered a feminine rune, it may work better for women.)

Hold the rune *Perdhro* in your hand.

This rune is connected with psychic ability and occult power. Whenever you want to encourage intuitive insights, hold an object on which the rune above is inscribed in your left hand and rub it.

Display the High Priestess card from the tarot deck in a place where you will see it often.

The High Priestess is the third card in the major arcana, and she represents intuition. What impressions come to you as you gaze at the symbols in this image? Look at this card often to stir your own intuition and remind you to pay attention to your psychic powers.

Display the Moon card from the tarot deck in a prominent place.

The Moon represents things hidden in the subconscious. When you gaze at this card, let its symbolism help you get in touch with your inner depths and bring subterranean material to the surface.

Eat cucumbers.

Ancient wise men and women believed you could improve psychic power by eating certain foods. If the adage "You are what you eat" is true, eating cucumbers, a vegetable linked with intuition and receptivity, can indeed enhance psychic ability.

Put cucumber slices over your eyelids during meditation.

This technique is both practical and esoteric. Cucumbers are believed to have properties that augment intuition. Placing cool, soothing circles of cucumber over your eyelids while meditating helps relax you, so you are more receptive to psychic impulses.

Listen to the ocean.

The ocean has long been a symbol of the emotions and the intuitive realm. The soothing sound of waves breaking on the shore can also stimulate development of a light trance state, during which you are more receptive to psychic impressions. If you don't live near the sea, listen to a recording of the sound of the ocean.

Listen to the "voice" inside a shell.

Conch shells are perfect for this exercise, but just about any large shell will do. Hold it to your left ear and listen to the sound coming from inside the shell. What is its message to you?

See orgone energy emanating from a body of water.

Austrian psychiatrist and biologist Wilhelm Reich proposed that a life energy, which he called "orgone," is concentrated in rivers, ponds, and other bodies of water. Sit quietly and let your mind drift as you gaze at a lake or pond. (Tip: It's easier to see orgone above still surfaces than above choppy water.) Look just above the surface of the water—can you see a faint, swirling movement that may appear bluish-white or slightly milky? That's orgone energy (also known as *ch'i* or prana).

Look at the symbol for Neptune.

In astrology, Neptune is the planet of visions and intuition. Draw the symbol below on a piece of paper and display it in a place where you can gaze at it when you want to stimulate your own intuitive powers. You may recognize this symbol as the trident carried by the god Neptune, ruler of the ocean.

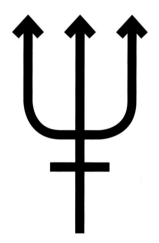

Listen to poetry.

Listening to poetry being read activates the right hemisphere of the brain—the part that houses intuition. Engaging in activities that stimulate and strengthen this hemisphere can encourage the development of your intuitive faculties.

Write poetry.

Choose a subject or experience that arouses some emotion in you and write a poem about it. Relax, keep an open mind, and just let the words flow. Don't censor yourself. Invite your inner self to participate in the process—you may be surprised by what transpires.

Take Bach flower remedies.

In the 1930s, the English physician Edward Bach determined that ingesting the distilled essenses of certain flowers can change emotional and psychic conditions. Taking the flower remedy Cerato helps develop a positive connection with your inner voice. (Note: Bach flower remedies and extracts bottled by other formulators can be purchased in most health-food stores and many new-age shops.)

Sense *ch'i* in your home.

In the Chinese art of placement known as feng shui, energy called *ch'i* is said to circulate through our homes and workplaces. Try to feel this energy in your own home. As you walk through the rooms, let your intuition sense the *ch'i* —where it feels heavy or sluggish, where it feels light or lively, where it seems tense or frenetic, and so on. (My book *10-Minute Feng Shui* is a good introduction to this popular subject.)

Sense *ch'i* in someone else's home.

Try to feel *ch'i* in a home you've never entered before. Pay attention to the clues your intuition gives you. If possible, check your impressions with the person who lives there or with a mutual friend to see if you interpreted the environmental energies correctly.

Gaze at the moon.

On the night of the full moon, place a large bowl of water outside where it will reflect the moon's image. Gaze at the reflection of the moon and let your mind relax. What impressions arise from the image in the water? How do you feel about these insights? (Note: If you live near a body of water, you may prefer to gaze at the moon's reflection in it.)

Sense the full moon.

The moon exerts a powerful influence on our planet—the changing tides clearly demonstrate this. Notice how you feel when the moon is full. Many people experience this as a time of increased energy and emotional sensitivity. Can you sense when the moon is full, even without looking at the sky or consulting a calendar?

Sense the new moon.

Pay attention to how you feel when the moon is new. Many people say they have less energy at this time; others feel more introspective or intuitive. Can you sense when the moon is new without looking at the sky or consulting a calendar?

Sense the moon's movement through the zodiac.

In astrology, the moon is linked with emotions and intuition. Every twenty-eight days, the moon completes its passage through all twelve signs of the zodiac, remaining in each sign for about two-and-a-half days. Can you sense its movement through the signs? Do you feel differently when the moon shifts from Pisces to Aries, for instance? Note your feelings, then consult an ephemeris, or astrological calendar, to see where the moon is positioned.

Have your aura photographed.

Special cameras are available for photographing auras, and you might find the colors you emanate fascinating. Your aura provides insight into your health, emotions, psychic ability, and how you express your energy.

Sense the image on a tarot card.

Choose a face-down tarot card from the deck. Without turning it over, see if you can intuit anything about it. Do you sense colors? Shapes? Images? Numbers? Can you identify the card? Turn it over and see how accurate your impressions were.

Sense a regular playing card.

If you don't have a tarot deck, you can use a regular poker deck. Choose a card and, without looking at it, try to intuit something about the card. Can you sense color? Shapes? A number?

Predict the weather.

Don't pay attention to the weather forecast for several days. See if you can predict the weather by noticing signs in nature or from other intuitive sources.

Pay attention to how your body communicates with you.

Your body often reveals information about your life situation that you may not consciously be aware of. This type of intuitive communication may involve physical symptoms or reactions. Is something giving you "a pain in the neck?" Are you having trouble "stomaching" something?

Talk to your body.

If you are experiencing pain, illness, or another physical problem, ask your body to tell you how to treat the problem. If you are unclear about what's causing the condition, ask your body for insight and guidance.

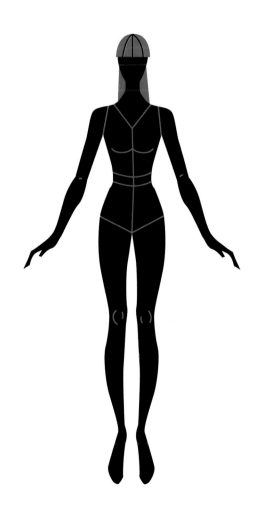

Create your own constellations.

Observe the stars on a clear night. Rather than connecting them to form the usual constellations, let your imagination make original shapes in the sky. What do these personal constellations mean to you?

Pay attention to your mental cycle.

According to the study of biorhythms, your mind functions on a thirty-three-day cycle. During half of this period, your mind is sharper and your memory is better; during the other half, your intuition is stronger.

Develop your intuition when Mercury is retrograde.

Astrologers connect Mercury with the mind. Every four months, Mercury goes "retrograde" for three weeks, when it appears to be moving backward in its orbit. During these periods, your rational intellect may not function as well as it usually does. However, your intuition might be stronger. This is an ideal time to work on developing your psychic skills by practicing the techniques outlined in this book.

Choose a shape.

Shapes have esoteric meanings as well as geometric ones. Let your intuition guide you to select a particular shape. This shape tells something about your situation at this time and/or what you need in your life. Squares relate to stability, circles to unity, rectangles to growth, triangles to movement and change, stars to protection, and straight lines to action.

Pick a color.

In the 1940s, Dr. Max Lüscher devised an interesting diagnostic test that relates personality to color preferences. Select a color without connecting it to anything else (such as clothing). This color describes how you are feeling or what you are looking for at this time. For instance, red relates to vitality, aggression, and passion; blue is linked with serenity; and pink, with love.

CH

5

DIVINATION

D ivination is the art of predicting the future, with or without the aid of special tools such as oracles. Also known as precognition, this psychic skill allows us to peek through the veil that separates the present from the future to see what lies ahead. The word *divination* "means allowing the divine to become manifest," explains Sarvananda Bluestone, Ph.D. "*Divination* is just another word for going beyond our ordinary awareness into the realms of the divine."

Since the beginning of time, people in cultures around the world have sought ways to see into the future in the hope of taking control of their lives. Our early ancestors relied on signs to survive. They understood the migratory patterns of birds and animals, the movements of the celestial bodies, and other natural occurrences. Thick coats on animals, for example, indicated that the coming winter would be cold. We still consult signs to foresee the future when we listen to a weather forecast.

Employing divination tools—astrology, runes, tarot cards, pendulums, and so on—is an ancient and time-honored practice. Many of the techniques discussed in this chapter involve the use of an oracle to predict upcoming events. I suggest you try more than one oracle—each has a slightly different way of communicating information, and you may simply like one form better than another. (In Chapter 3, I discuss these methods in greater detail.)

The techniques in this chapter fall into two general categories. Some strengthen your receptive and perceptive skills to help you see what lies ahead. Others improve your projective abilities so you can influence the course of future events.

Pay attention to hunches.

If you have a hunch or gut feeling about something, don't just shrug it off. Write it down and see if it comes to pass. Once you start paying attention to psychic impressions, they'll occur with greater frequency and your ability to understand them will improve.

Pay attention to recurring incidents.

Recurring incidents may be signs intended to get your attention. If you notice certain things happening more frequently—finding coins on the street, stubbing your toe, or misplacing your keys, for example—stop and pay attention. Your inner guidance may be trying to get through to you.

Watch animals and birds.

Some spiritual traditions hold that animals sometimes appear to alert you to matters or situations that will soon require your attention. If you see an animal, bird, or reptile—especially one that you aren't accustomed to seeing in your area—it could be a sign. Consider the characteristics associated with that animal, as they are the qualities you'll need to handle the situation. For instance, swans signify grace, lions denote courage, and foxes are associated with cleverness.

Use a pendulum to predict the future.

To learn about something that will occur in the near future, hold a pendulum loosely between your thumb and index finger and ask a question that can be answered with a yes or no response. Allow the pendulum to swing by itself. If it swings back and forth, the answer is yes. If it swings from side to side, the answer is no.

Use a pendulum to see how an action will affect you.

A pendulum can provide insight into a job, investment, or other matter that you are considering. Hold the pendulum loosely between your thumb and index finger and ask how a situation will affect you. Allow the pendulum to move by itself. If it swings in a clockwise circle, the situation is advantageous. If the pendulum swings in a counterclockwise circle, the situation is likely to be unfavorable.

Use a pendulum to see how someone will respond to you.

Hold the pendulum loosely between your thumb and index finger and ask how someone will respond if you take a certain course of action. Allow the pendulum to move by itself. If it swings in a clockwise circle, the person's response will be favorable. If the pendulum swings in a counterclockwise circle, his or her response will be unfavorable.

Pick a rune.

Close your eyes and mix up the runes in your set. Ask a question about something in the near future, then select a rune. Look up the meaning of the rune in Chapter 3 to discover the answer to your question.

Pick three runes.

Close your eyes and mix up the runes. Ask a question about something in the future, then select three runes. The first rune will represent the past, the second will symbolize the present, and the third will show what to expect in the near future.

Pick four runes.

Close your eyes and mix up the runes. Ask a question about something in the future, then select four runes. The first will represent the situation at present, the second will show the obstacle facing you. The third rune will suggest he action you should take to overcome the obstacle, and the fourth will reveal the outcome that is likely to occur in the near future.

Cast three runes.

Ask a yes-or-no question about something in the near future while you mix up the runes. Select three runes, then gently toss them onto a tabletop or other surface. If two or three of the runes fall right side up, the answer is yes. If two or three runes fall upside down, the answer is no.

Look for runes in nature.

Because Norse rune symbols are very simple line configurations, you can spot them in many places—a crack in a rock, or the way a tree's branches intersect, for instance. Contemplate an issue whose future progress or outcome you want to know more about. Go outside and gaze around until you notice a naturally occurring pattern in the shape of a rune. This is your answer or guidance. (The meanings of the runes can be found in Chapter 3.)

Let an "accidental" rune set the tone for the day.

Each morning, start the day by going outside with an open mind and casting your eyes about until you spot a rune. This might appear as a symbol on a traffic sign, a crack in the sidewalk, or a shape formed by metalwork on a bridge. Let this pattern set the tone for the day. (Look up the meanings of the runes in Chapter 3 or in a book about runes.)

Pick a tarot card.

Shuffle a deck of tarot cards while contemplating a question about something in the near future. When you feel ready, close your eyes and select one card. The card will provide insight or guidance related to your question. (For a key to the meanings of the individual cards, refer to Chapter 3.)

Pick three cards.

Shuffle a tarot deck while contemplating a question about something in the near future. Choose three cards. The first card will describe the situation in the past, the second card will tell what's happening now, and the third card will show what the future is likely to bring. (Tip: This type of reading usually can provide information only about things that are likely to transpire within a month or so. For information about the meanings of the individual cards, refer to Chapter 3.)

Pick four cards.

Shuffle a tarot deck while thinking about a question or situation. Choose four cards. The first card will describe the situation as it exists now. The second card will show what the obstacle facing you is. The third card will offer advice about what action you should take to overcome the obstacle, and the fourth card will reveal the outcome that will take place in the near future.

How many cards are from the major arcana?

The major arcana cards suggest that "fate" or forces outside your control are influencing the situation you are inquiring about (see Chapter 3 for more information and brief interpretations). If half (or more) of the cards you drew are from the major arcana, you may not have much control over how the situation will unfold in the future.

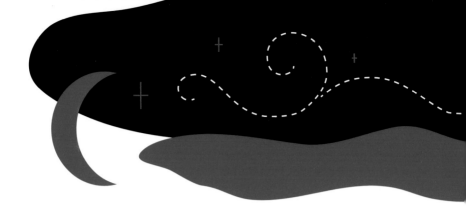

Pay attention to dream symbols.

Note any poignant symbols or images that appear in your dreams—these symbols may be indicators of things to come. (For more information about dreams, see Chapter 1.)

Notice dreams about water.

Water symbolizes our emotions. A dream about water may predict an emotional situation that will occur in the near future. Notice if the water is clear, calm, murky, icy, or turbulent—its condition could signify the nature of the emotional situation you will soon face.

Notice dreams about houses.

A house in a dream symbolizes your life. Notice the condition of the house—is it run-down or palatial? Cluttered or spacious? Are there any rooms you haven't explored yet? Your inner guidance may be using the imagery of a house to give you advice about the state of your life and how to proceed in the future.

Pay attention to dreams that occur on your birthday.

Dreams that occur on your birthday are likely to have special significance. They may presage experiences in the upcoming year or offer valuable insights.

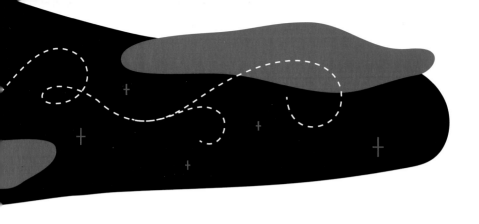

Notice numbers in dreams.

Numbers have symbolic meanings as well as quantitative values. If you dream of a number, it may be a signal about something in the future that you need to be aware of. A dream that includes the number 1 may predict a new beginning, for example. (See Chapter 3 for more information about numbers.)

Keep a dream log.

Each morning, write down your dreams in detail, especially the ones that are particularly vivid or emotional. Make sure to date your dreams. Periodically review what you recorded to see if anything in your dreams came to pass. In this manner, you'll gradually train yourself to recognize dream symbols and determine when a dream is actually a premonition.

Notice animals in your dreams.

Animals may appear in your dreams in order to guide you or give you information about an upcoming situation. The characteristics embodied by this animal, bird, or reptile are qualities you can use to handle the situation.

Gaze into a crystal ball.

Allow your mind to relax as you gaze into a crystal ball. Imagine that you are seeing the future in the glossy surface. Don't try to focus too clearly—let your vision blur a bit as you wait for impressions to come. What do you see? What do you feel? How do you interpret your impressions? (Note: A genuine quartz crystal ball is a better scrying tool than one made of leaded crystal or clear glass.)

Gaze into a flame.

This technique is similar to the one above. Whether you stare at a roaring fire or a burning candle, the dancing flame causes your mind to relax and slip into a trancelike state. Imagine you are watching the future unfold in the flickering firelight. What do you see and feel? What do these impressions mean to you?

Gaze at a blank TV screen.

Turn off the television and look at the blank screen. Let your mind relax. Watch as images that portray the future gradually appear on the screen. What do these images reveal to you?

Stare at the moon.

The moon is linked with the unconscious, intuition, and the psychic realm. Go outside at night and gaze up at the moon, as if it were a scrying device. What do you see in the moon's enigmatic face? What do these impressions tell you about the future?

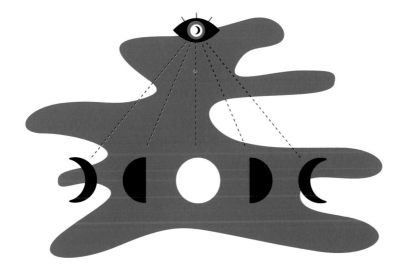

Let the waxing moon influence your future.

The moon's waxing cycle (the period between the new and full moons) is a time of increase. You can use this lunar energy to encourage growth in a particular area of your life in the near future. This is the time to begin a project, make an investment, or plant "seeds" that you want to grow.

Let the waning moon influence your future.

The moon's waning cycle (between full and new) is a time of decrease. You can use this lunar energy to influence decline in a particular matter in the near future. This is the time to begin a diet, clean out your closets, or end an unfulfilling relationship.

Check your numerological year cycle.

Your "personal year" runs from birthday to birthday, not from January 1 to December 31. Add together the number of your birth month, your day of birth, and the four digits of the coming year. Then reduce the result by adding the digits together until you arrive at a single number. This number shows what the next year holds for you. (See Chapter 3 for a key to each number and to learn more about numerology.)

Check your numerological month cycle.

After you've determined the single-digit number of your next personal year, you can see what each month within that year will be like. Add the number of the month to the number of your personal year and reduce the sum to a single digit; then turn to Chapter 3 for a key to the numbers.

Sit under a tree.

Trees have long been viewed as sources of wisdom. The Buddha sat under a tree to gain knowledge and enlightenment. The Norse god Odin, who brought the runes to humankind, hung on the great tree Yggdrasil for nine days. The Tree of Life forms the foundation of Kabbalistic belief. The Druids saw trees as sacred embodiments of certain qualities; their World Tree served as a link between the worlds. Sit quietly under a tree and let it communicate its wisdom to you. What does it tell you about the future?

Climb a tree.

Relax, close your eyes, and take a few deep breaths. Imagine you are crawling into a hole at the base of a tree, near the roots. In your mind's eye, see yourself climbing up inside the tree's trunk until you notice an opening near the top. Move toward the opening—when you emerge from it, you'll have a better vantage point from which to see the future.

Ride an elevator to the top floor.

This is a more modern version of the shamanic exercise above. Relax, close your eyes, and take a few deep breaths. Imagine you are entering an elevator in a skyscraper. Push a button and ride all the way up to the top floor. When the doors open, you emerge into the future. What does it look like?

Take a walk into the future.

This exercise is similar to the one above. Relax, close your eyes, and imagine that you are walking along a road that leads from the present to the future. As you journey down this road, you'll see things that will come true in time. The farther you travel down the road, the more distant the events. (Note: Things that are far off in the future may change, depending on the actions you take.)

Toss three coins.

Hold three coins in your hand while you ask a yes-or-no question, then toss the coins on a flat surface. If more coins fall "heads" up, your answer is yes. If more fall "tails" up, the answer is no.

Ask a daisy for advice.

Pick a daisy and ask a yes-or-no question. Pull the petals off one by one. Instead of saying "he loves me, he loves me not" as you remove petals, say "yes, no, yes, no" until you get down to the last petal, which is your answer.

Use a Ouija board.

Although Ouija boards have developed a bad image because of horror shows, they are simply devices for tapping into your subconscious or opening up your mind so you can receive messages from other sources. You can consult a Ouija board alone or with another person. Relax and place your fingertips lightly on the sensing device, known as a planchette. Ask a question about the future. Let the planchette slide around on the board by itself—don't try to influence its movement—as it responds to your question.

Get an *I Ching* reading online.

Various websites offer free *I Ching* readings. Many of these are quite accurate and informative. Try a few and see what they can tell you about the future.

Use a Scrabble set to divine the future.

Mix up the letters in a Scrabble set while contemplating a situation about which you'd like to know the progress or outcome. When you are ready, draw as many letters as you wish. Turn them over and make a word or anagram from them. What information does this word give you in the context of your concern?

Pick a word.

You can use a set of refrigerator-magnet words for this exercise, or cut out words from a magazine. Without looking, mix up the words while contemplating something in the future you want information about. Then draw a word and reflect on its meaning in the context of your concern.

Form a sentence.

This exercise expands on the one above. After mixing up your words and asking a question about the future, draw several words. Look at the words you chose and form a phrase or sentence with them. If you prefer, form the phrase or sentence before you look at the words. Your subconscious might construct a "phrase" that has special meaning to you, even if the arrangement of the words seems nonsensical to other people.

Pull a wishbone.

A wish that's made with sincerity can influence your future and attract good fortune to you. Dry a wishbone from a turkey or chicken. Hold one end while another person holds the other. Make a wish with clear intention and create a mental image of the outcome you desire. Pull the wishbone apart until it breaks—the person who gets the longer piece will receive his or her wish.

Make a wish list.

List up to ten things that you want to happen in the coming year. Post your list in a place where you'll see it often. By focusing attention on this list, you pave the way for these wishes to manifest themselves in your life.

Blow out candles on your birthday cake.

Like the above exercise, this one uses your intention to influence the future. Light the candles on a cake, then clearly visualize a wish you want to come true as you blow out the candles.

Wish on a star.

If you see a falling star, wish for something you want to occur in the future. Be sure to make your wish with sincerity and clarity so the energy you project can help create the conditions you want.

Be careful of what you wish for.

Phrase your wish carefully and make sure you are clear in your own mind about what you want—you are likely to get exactly what you ask for, so be sure to cover all your bases.

Pay attention to the first thought you have upon waking.

The first thought that comes into your mind upon waking may set the tone for the day or convey information that could be useful to you during the day.

Pay attention to the first thing you hear upon waking.

The first sound you hear (other than your alarm clock) could be a sign that has relevance to upcoming events or experiences.

Change your perception to change the future.

We influence situations with our emotions, thoughts, and reactions. If you want to change the outcome of a particular situation, try changing your perception of it or the way you think, feel, or act in connection with it. By changing the present, you change the future.

Notice physical sensations.

Do your ears burn when someone is talking about you? Do you get a chill on the back of your neck when your spirit guide sends you a message? Pay attention to physical sensations, as well as to what you are thinking or doing at the time you experience these sensations. They could be signs that are intended to guide you.

Notice emotions connected with physical signs.

Your feelings can be clues to the significance of a particular sign. Notice how you feel when you receive a sign—optimistic, anxious, guarded, eager. Do you experience an "Aha!"? Do different feelings accompany different signs?

Keep a log of signs and outcomes.

Record your signs and what transpires in connection with them. This will help you determine which signs are true indicators of upcoming situations and which have other purposes. It will also encourage your subconscious and other sources to continue communicating with you.

Use tarot cards to answer a question about the future, exercise 1.

Shuffle a deck of tarot cards while you contemplate a yes-or-no question regarding something in the future that you want information about. When you are ready, draw three cards from the deck and turn them face up. If more cards are upright, the answer is yes. If more cards are upside down, the answer is no.

Use tarot cards to answer a question about the future, exercise 2.

Shuffle a deck of tarot cards while you contemplate a yes-or-no question regarding something in the future that you want to know more about. When you are ready, begin turning cards from the top of the deck face up in a pile until you either turn up an ace or have thirteen cards in your pile. Start a second pile and do the same thing—stop when you get an ace or have turned up thirteen cards. Make a third pile in the same manner. If you have turned up two or three aces and the aces are upright, the answer is yes. If the aces are upside down, the answer is no. If one ace is upright and one is upside down, the situation can go either way. If you have only one ace or none, an answer cannot be determined at this time.

Use regular playing cards to answer a question about the future.

If you don't have a tarot deck, you can use regular playing cards in the same manner that was described above. The odds will change, however. Because most tarot decks have seventy-eight cards and poker decks have only fifty-two, you are more likely to get aces and thus receive a definitive answer. (Note: Before shuffling the deck, find the ace of diamonds and mark the "bottom" of the card so you'll know whether it's upright or upside down.)

Make a divining stick.

Turn a four-sided stick, such as a chopstick, into a "divining stick." On one side, write, "Go forward." Write "Wait a while" on another side. On the third side, write, "Enlist another's help" and on the fourth side write, "Retreat." Hold the stick between your hands while you contemplate a situation that you want advice about. Then toss the stick and read the answer on the upright side.

Use a divining circle to see what lies ahead.

Draw a circle of about ten inches in diameter and mark an X inside to divide the circle into four quadrants. Lay this on a flat surface. Cast a stone onto the circle. If it lands in the upper quadrant, a time of decrease lies ahead. If the stone lands in the bottom quadrant, the future will bring growth. A new beginning is signaled if the stone lands in the quadrant to your right. Something will be ending soon if the stone lands in the quadrant to your left.

Cast a rune into a divining circle.

First, with your left hand, mix up the runes while contemplating a question or situation you want to know more about. Randomly choose one rune, close your eyes, and cast it onto the divining circle divided into quadrants, as described above. Refer to the list of rune interpretations in Chapter 3 for insight into the question or situation. The quadrant into which the rune falls shows how the situation is likely to turn out.

Cast a rune on a birth chart.

This technique combines two divination systems, runes and astrology. First, close your eyes and consider a situation you want to know more about. With your eyes still closed, choose a rune and cast it on your birth chart. Which of the twelve houses did it fall in? The combined meanings of this house and the rune you selected answer your question. (Note: Consult a book on astrology to learn the meaning of each house in the chart.)

Use the rune *Kenaz* to attract good luck in the future.

This rune helps you open yourself on a psychic level to receive good things in the future. Draw the symbol below on a piece of paper and display it where you will see it often to serve as a visual reminder of your intention.

Carry *Kenaz* in your pocket.

If you prefer, you can carry in your pocket a rune stone that bears the symbol below. Touch it often to send into the cosmic web psychic vibes that will help you attract good luck in the future.

Pay attention to "random" thoughts.

When thoughts pop into your head unbidden, take notice and see what may have inspired them. Some thoughts may be messages from your subconscious or another source, alerting you to something that you should prepare for.

Read tea leaves.

Brew a cup of tea using loose tea, rather than a tea bag, while you contemplate a situation or question about which you seek information or advice for the future. Carefully drink or pour out the liquid, leaving the wet leaves sticking to the bottom of the cup. Gaze at the pattern made by the leaves—what does it say to you?

Consult the four directions.

Think about a situation or question about which you seek information or advice for the future. Toss a pointed stick into the air. Notice which direction it points when it lands. If it points north, you should pull back or avoid making changes; if it points south, go forward or take action. If the stick falls with its point to the east, this is the time to try something new or to expand. If it falls pointing west, you are advised to let go of something or cut back. If you cannot decide which direction the stick points toward the most, toss the stick again.

Pick a numbered card.

Remove the jacks, queens, and kings from a deck of playing cards. Shuffle the cards while contemplating a question about the future. Choose a card, then look up that number's meaning in the key given for tarot cards numbered 1 through 10 in Chapter 3. The number suggests how you should proceed or how your situation is likely to turn out.

Plan around eclipses.

If you begin something on the day of an eclipse, you are likely to see further development of that matter during future eclipses.

Make predictions by eclipses.

Eclipses often serve as catalysts, activating situations or bringing matters to light. Look ahead to the dates for eclipses to anticipate movement or change in a situation.

CH

6

OTHER PEOPLE

N o man is an island, as the poet John Donne once wrote. We must all learn to live and work with other people. The more we understand about those with whom we come into contact, the better our chances are for establishing harmonious, mutually rewarding relationships.

Ordinary interactive skills and observations serve us well in many aspects of our social relations. Most of the time, we can get along just fine by using oral and written communication. I doubt telepathy will replace conversation anytime in the foreseeable future. And I suspect that our personal experiences with friends and associates will continue to be the basis on which we form our opinions of them. But we can definitely expand our insights into other people—and ourselves—by drawing upon our psychic powers in our interpersonal interactions.

The techniques in this chapter require the participation of at least one other person. Although you can have fun doing them, they are not parlor games. Exercises in the first section are designed to help you and a partner (or group) strengthen your mind-reading and projective powers. The second section offers tips for gaining instant insight into the people you know—their character traits, motivations, strengths and weaknesses, even secrets you might not have discovered otherwise.

As you work with these techniques, you'll discover that your "mental muscles" grow stronger. I recommend that you try them all, for the various exercises target different areas of your mind, just as different Nautilus machines tone various parts of your body. After a while, you may find that some of the techniques are of more use to you than are others and opt to eliminate the less effective ones.

MENTAL TELEPATHY

Pay attention to your first impression of a person.

Your first impressions tell you a lot about someone—this response is how your intuition communicates information to you. The next time you meet someone new, pay attention to your first impressions. As you get to know the person better, see how many of your first impressions were correct. If you don't get to know the person better, check with a mutual friend to see if your intuitions were accurate.

Contact another person telepathically.

Start thinking about someone you know. Mentally call his or her name or visualize the person's face. Focus all your attention on the person for brief periods of time throughout the day or over a span of several days, if necessary. See how long it takes for the person to contact you.

Communicate with someone at a distance.

Sit quietly, close your eyes, and still your mind. Imagine you are sitting in the middle of a circle. Now call to mind the image of someone you want to communicate with and see him or her sitting before you, in the center of another circle. Visualize a beam of blue light connecting your forehead with the other person's forehead. When you've established this link, communicate mentally with him or her. Afterwards, you may wish to call the person and ask if your message was received.

Receive telepathic communication from another person.

If you feel a strong urge to contact someone you know, or if that person keeps popping into your head for no apparent reason—especially if it's someone you haven't spoken to recently—note the date and time of each impression. Then contact that individual and ask if he or she has been trying to reach you. Do the times you noted concur with the times the other person was thinking about you?

Communicate through a rope.

Sit facing another person, about six feet apart. Hold one end of a rope and ask your partner to hold the other end. The rope acts as a conductor for your thoughts. Form a clear thought in your mind, then send it through the rope to your partner. Can he or she read you? Do you "feel" mental vibrations traveling along the rope?

Communicate with a friend through a crystal.

Crystals are known for their ability to store information—that's why they're used in computers. Close your eyes and form an image in your mind. Hold a piece of natural quartz crystal to your "third eye" and project the image into the crystal. Give the crystal to a friend and ask him or her to try to intuit the image you put in it.

Contact someone on the "other side."

Has someone you love crossed to the "other side"? Try to contact him or her, using the same projective techniques you've already practiced with friends in this world.

Project shapes to another person.

Special cards called "Zener" cards with shapes on them are often used in telepathy. You can make your own by drawing a circle on one index card, a square on another, a cross on a third, a star on the fourth, and wavy lines on the last card. Then, concentrate on one card at a time while your partner tries to guess which shape you're looking at.

Perceive shapes sent by someone else.

Now switch places with your partner and let him or her focus attention on the different shapes. See if you can read your partner's mind.

Project colors to another person.

Some people are better at sensing colors than shapes. Draw a box on one side of each of six index cards. Color each box a different color—red, orange, yellow, green, blue, and purple. Concentrate on one card at a time while your partner tries to guess which color you're looking at.

Perceive colors sent by someone else.

Now switch places with your partner and let him or her focus attention on the different colors. Are you better at picking up colors or shapes?

Project pictures to another person.

Once you've mastered colors and shapes, try to project a more complex image to your partner. Tarot cards are ideal for this, but if you prefer, you can use photos or pictures from a magazine. Concentrate on a picture you've selected while the other person tries to pick up the image you are looking at. Your partner may get an impression of colors or shapes—or even the entire image.

Perceive images sent by a partner.

Exchange places and let your partner send images to you. How much of the picture can you pick up?

Project thoughts about food to a partner.

The more senses you can connect with a thought, the stronger the transmission of that thought will be. Think about a food you like. Imagine not only the way it looks, but how it smells, how it feels to chew it, and what tastes it brings to your tongue. Project all these sensory images to your partner. Can he or she identify the food?

Perceive images of food.

Change roles and ask your friend to project sensory images of a favorite food to you. How much can you pick up?

Find out whom your partner is thinking about.
Ask a partner to think of someone you both know well. Can you read your partner's mind and identify this mutual friend or acquaintance?

Project your thoughts to your partner.
Switch places and think about someone you both know well. Can your partner tell whom you're thinking about?

Read impressions from another person's jewelry.
This common example of psychometry works because gemstones and metals hold on to a person's energetic material for a long time. Jewelry that is worn frequently is the easiest to read. Hold a piece of jewelry in your hand and quiet your mind. Allow impressions to arise into your awareness without censoring them. What feelings or images do you pick up?

Identify people from their possessions.
Collect personal objects, such as jewelry, from at least six people. These should be items that don't obviously identify the person to whom they belong—no monograms, family crests, or the like. Can you connect the object with its owner simply by sensing its vibrations?

What colors are your friends?

Do this exercise with at least five friends. Without letting you see it, each person selects a crayon that describes him or her, writes his or her name on a piece of paper with it, and returns it to the box. When everyone has finished, try to guess which friend is which color. How many did you get right? (Note: Have your friends choose their crayons from a box that contains at least sixteen colors.)

What animals are your friends?

Do this exercise with at least five friends. Ask each friend to secretly choose an animal with which she or he feels a certain kinship. Have each person draw a quick sketch of his or her "totem" animal. When everyone has finished, try to guess which friend is which animal, then look at their drawings. How many did you get right?

Sense another person's presence, technique 1.

This technique helps sensitize your aura. With your eyes closed, stand about three feet away from another person. Ask your partner to reach out toward you, without making any noise or touching your physical body, whenever he or she chooses. When you feel your partner's fingers brush your aura, say, "Now." Open your eyes and see if you correctly identified the point at which he or she "touched" you.

Sense another person's presence, technique 2.

This technique is a more intense version of the previous exercise. Ask a partner to stand about five feet (1.5 m) away from you. Close your eyes. Ask your partner to slowly walk toward you, without making any noise. When you feel him or her come in contact with your aura, say, "Now." How close did your partner get before you sensed his or her presence?

Feel a friend's aura.

While a friend sits with his or her eyes closed, hold your palms a few inches above this person's head. Don't actually touch your friend's physical body. Can you feel his or her aura? Can your friend feel your hands?

Touch someone psychically.

Once you've mastered the previous techniques, try this more advanced one. Close your eyes and imagine your body expanding until it "touches" your partner, who is sitting on the other side of the room. Ask your partner to let you know when he or she feels your psychic touch.

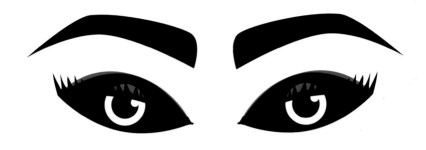

Give someone "the eye."

Most of us can sense when someone is looking at us. The next time you are in a public place, stare at and focus your attention on someone whose back is to you. How quickly does the person feel your gaze? This exercise strengthens your powers of mental projection.

Sense someone looking at you.

Close your eyes while a partner stares at some part of your body. Can you guess what part he or she is looking at?

Sense colored light projected at you.

Once you've mastered the previous technique, take it a step further. Ask your partner to mentally project at you a beam of colored light. Can you sense what color it is?

Send healing energy to someone you know.

Relax, close your eyes, and imagine someone you know who is ill, injured, or in need of some type of healing. Visualize bright green light—the color of health and growth—surrounding this person or concentrated on a specific part of his or her body. Hold this image in your mind for as long as you can. (Note: Make sure to ask the person's permission before performing this psychic healing technique.)

Send psychic protection to someone you know.

Relax, close your eyes, and imagine someone you know who needs some extra protection while traveling, for instance. Visualize that person surrounded by a cocoon of pure white light. Hold this image in your mind for as long as you wish, until you sense the person's security is ensured.

Pick a hand.

Once you master this technique, you'll always get to go first in chess, checkers, and other games. Ask a partner to conceal a white chess piece in one hand and a black one in the other. Try to pick the hand holding the white piece. Repeat this exercise ten times and keep track of the number of your "hits."

Find a concealed crystal.

This technique is a little like a "shell game," except the intent is to strengthen your psychic ability rather than to trick you. Ask a partner to place a piece of quartz crystal under one of three paper cups while you keep your eyes closed. Can you sense where the crystal is hidden?

Focusing, exercise 1.

This technique hones your ability to focus—an essential part of projecting mental messages to another person. Ask a partner to place ten different objects on a table. Look at them for thirty seconds before your partner covers them up or removes them. How many can you remember?

Remove one of the items.

Ask your partner to remove one of the ten items as you look away. Can you tell which one is missing?

Focusing, exercise 2.

This technique is a slightly more difficult version of focusing exercise 1. Ask a partner to make a list of ten different items. Read through the list, then give it back to your partner. How many of the items can you remember?

Focusing, exercise 3.

Leave the room while your partner changes something in it. When you return, can you discern what has changed?

Guess what card you're holding, exercise 1.

Sit in a circle with a group of at least five other people. One of you shuffles a deck of cards, then deals one card face down to each person. Without looking at your cards, hold them up to your foreheads, face side out, so that the other people in the circle can see them—you can see everyone else's cards, but not your own. Try to intuit whether your card is higher than the others' cards.

Guess what card you're holding, exercise 2.

When you've mastered the previous technique, try this more difficult one. Shuffle and deal one card face down to each person in the circle. Don't look at your card or pick it up—just hold your hands over it. Can you intuit whose card is highest?

Ring a bell.

Ask a friend to ring a bell at random intervals. Each time you hear the bell, it will stimulate your psychic perception. Note what thoughts were in your mind just before you heard the bell and what impressions came to you immediately afterwards.

Sense the object of a partner's attention, exercise 1.

Arrange five objects on a table. Ask a partner to focus all of his or her attention on one of the objects. Can you guess which one it is?

Sense the object of a partner's attention, exercise 2.

After you've mastered the previous exercise, try this more advanced technique. Ask a partner to think intently about an object in the room. Can you identify the object?

Sense the object of a group's attention.

Now perform the above technique with a group. Ask everyone to concentrate on the same object. Is it easier to identify the object when many people focus their attention on it?

Recognize your rock.

Ask five (or more) friends to join you in doing this exercise. Give each person a small rock of about the same size, shape, and color. After they've all taken a few moments to "bond" with their rocks, collect and mark them in a way that your friends won't be able to see (for instance, by chalking a number on the bottom). Place all the rocks together in a group. Can everyone identify his or her own rock by feeling its vibrations?

Use teamwork to make a flame flicker.

Sometimes two minds are better than one. Ask a friend—or a group of
people—to join you in focusing all your attention on a candle flame. Try
to make the flame flicker. (Note: Make sure the candle isn't near a draft or
anything else that would affect the movement of the flame.)

Make water ripple.

Like the exercise above, this one uses the combined power of two or more
minds to produce a physical phenomenon. Fill a saucer or shallow bowl with
water and set it on a table. Concentrate together on producing a ripple on the
surface of the water by using only your minds to generate movement.

Sense what's in a letter.

Ask a friend to write you a short letter containing no more than three different pieces of information or topics. Without opening the letter, try to intuit the contents. Then, open the envelope and see if you were correct.

Drum a message to another person.

Before we had telephones and e-mail, drums were used in many parts of the world to send messages. Translate an idea or feeling into drumbeats and play this message to a friend. Can he or she understand your message?

Receive a drum message.

Switch places and listen with your intuition as your partner drums a message to you. Can you understand what he or she is saying?

Identify someone psychically, exercise 1.

Get together with three (or more) other people. Sit or stand with your eyes closed while your friends move around the room. After a few moments, have one person approach you and brush your hands lightly with his or her hands. Can you identify this person by touch alone?

Identify someone psychically, exercise 2.

After doing the above exercise, try to identify the person who approaches you without having him or her touch you. What clues can you use?

Synchronize your clocks.

With a group of friends, agree that tomorrow you will all set your clocks to a certain time—but don't discuss with each other at what time you'll make that change. How close did you come to synchronizing your clocks?

Select a piece of music.

See if you and a group of friends are on the same wavelength. Agree that each of you will play a particular piece of music at a designated time. Don't discuss the music you'll play—wait until the appointed time to decide, then let your intuition guide you. Did you all choose classical music? Jazz? Country? Pieces by the same artist? Even the same song?

READING OTHER PEOPLE

Look at someone's thumb.

In hand analysis, the thumb relates to the ego, or sense of self. A person who has a large thumb has a big ego and likes to be the center of attention. A person with a small thumb lacks self-confidence or may be very shy. (For more information about hand analysis, see Chapter 3.)

Check the "moons" on another person's fingernails.

If the person's nails contain large white "moons" rising near the cuticle, he or she has plenty of natural vitality.

Examine the shape of a person's fingernails.

Round nails indicate that the person is friendly and outgoing; square nails show that he or she is practical and handy. Long, narrow fingernails identify a creative and intuitive individual. Trapezoid-shaped nails reveal an adventurous sort of person. (Note: Consider only the pinkish part of the nail that's attached to the finger, not the whitish part at the end.)

Look at the spaces between someone's fingers.

Ask a person to place his or her hands, palms down, on a tabletop. If there are wide spaces between the fingers, the person is likely to be outgoing, impulsive, open, and daring. If the fingers are held close together, he or she is cautious, conservative, and reserved.

Test the flexibility in a friend's fingers.

Gently bend a friend's fingers back and forth. The degree of flexibility in the fingers shows how rigid or adaptable the person is in life.

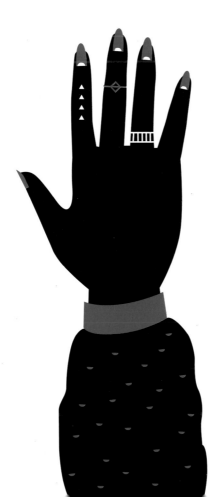

Study a person's love line.

The love line is the one that's nearest the fingers on most people's palms. If it is straight, the person approaches relationships in a practical, controlled manner. If it curves upward, that person is idealistic and romantic.

Look at someone's head line.

The head line is the middle line on most palms, and it runs horizontally across the palm from between the thumb and index finger toward the outside of the hand. If this line is straight, it suggests a person whose thinking is rational and orderly. If the line curves downward in the direction of the wrist, however, the person is driven by emotions.

Examine the skin on the backs of a person's hands.

Thick, coarse skin with large pores indicates that the person is rather tough and insensitive—"thick-skinned." Delicate skin with almost invisible pores suggests that the person is quite fragile and sensitive—a "hothouse flower."

Compare the skin on a person's hands and face.

Sometimes there is a distinct difference between the quality of the skin on someone's face and that on the backs of his or her hands. Facial skin denotes the outer personality, the "face" this individual shows to the world. The skin on the hands reveals what the person is really like inside.

See the aura around a person's head.

The aura is a subtle energy field that surrounds the physical body. If you look carefully, you can see it glowing like a faint halo around a person's head—especially if that person is standing against a dark background. A bright, clear, light-colored aura indicates good vitality and a healthy attitude. A dark, murky one suggests the person is experiencing some sort of emotional upset or perhaps health problems. (See Chapter 1 for more information about auras.)

Notice changes in a person's aura.

When our emotions change, our auras reflect the change. Observe a friend's aura when he or she is experiencing strong emotions—anger, joy, fear, sadness, excitement, stress, and so on. Can you detect differences in your friend's aura?

Take a photo of someone's aura.

Auras can sometimes be captured on film. Special cameras and techniques are available for this purpose, but you may be able to photograph a friend's aura with a cell phone camera, 35-mm, or digital camera. (Tip: Seat your subject in front of a black background.)

Photograph a friend's emotions.

Because strong emotions are reflected in our auras, you may be able to photograph changes in a friend's aura during a period of intense emotion. Even if you weren't able to film his or her aura during normal circumstances, you might capture it now.

Read a friend's emotions.

We often sense other people's emotional states because powerful emotions charge the environment around us. Ask a friend to relive an emotional experience without telling you what he or she is feeling. Close your eyes and tune in to your friend's emotions. Can you feel what your friend feels?

Send an emotional response to a partner.

After doing the above exercise, switch roles. Now it's your turn to relive an emotional experience. Can your partner pick up the vibes you're emitting?

Hold a friend's hand.

Our hands reveal a lot about us. Hold a friend's hand and try to tune in to his or her energy field. What does your friend's hand tell you about him or her?

Read a stranger from a handshake.

A person's handshake reveals a lot about him or her. The next time you meet someone new, notice your response to that person's handshake. A limp handshake may indicate an unwillingness to connect with you. A vigorous handshake may mean the person is overly concerned about making a good impression. Pay attention to your responses, then check them out with a mutual friend.

Discuss your dreams with a friend.

Sometimes a friend can offer a different perspective on or insight into your dreams that you might have missed. Discussing your dreams can also prompt greater recall.

Meditate with other people.

Our energies affect those of other people. Therefore, meditating with a partner or group may help you deepen your trance or increase the power of the positive vibrations you activate during meditation.

What's in a name?

Assign number values to the vowels in another person's name, as explained in the numerology section of Chapter 3. Add the numbers together and reduce them to a single digit, then refer to the numerology chart to see what that person is really like inside.

Discover a friend's life purpose.

Assign number values to all the letters in a friend's full name, as explained in Chapter 3. Add the numbers together and reduce them to a single digit. Refer to the numerology chart to see what that person's purpose is in life.

Discover a person's life lesson.

The date of someone's birth shows what his or her lesson in life is. Add the numbers of the birth month, day, and year together and reduce that sum to a single digit. Then refer to the chart in Chapter 3 to see what lesson he or she is supposed to learn in this lifetime.

Look at someone's birth chart.

A person's birth chart is a cryptic snapshot of him or her. Even if you aren't an astrologer, you can intuit information about someone by gazing at his or her chart. Let your mind grow calm and just look at the diagram, allowing impressions to rise into your awareness. Then, check your psychic impulses to see how many were correct.

Was the person born under the zodiac sign Aries?

Aries people are assertive, independent, and impatient. Easily bored, they need lots of activity and challenges in both their personal and professional lives. They are better at starting things than finishing them. (See Chapter 3 for more about astrology. My book *Planets in Signs* provides in-depth information about zodiac signs and personality.)

Was the person born under the zodiac sign Taurus?

Taurus people are easygoing, down-to-earth, and creative. Practical and stubborn, they pursue their goals slowly and steadily. These indulgent and sensual individuals enjoy life's luxuries—good food, music, art, and sex.

Was the person born under the zodiac sign Gemini?

Geminis are idea people who invest their energy in learning, communicating, and sharing information with others. Sociable and talkative, they usually have many friends and acquaintances with whom they enjoy a variety of interests.

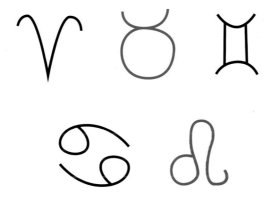

Was the person born under the zodiac sign Cancer?

Home and family are very important to Cancers. They are compassionate and nurturing people who enjoy caring for others. Sensitive and emotional, Cancers need to feel secure, both financially and in relationships.

Was the person born under the zodiac sign Leo?

Dramatic Leos are born actors and enjoy being the center of attention. Many of them are quite creative and possess artistic talent of some kind. These proud, charismatic, and self-confident individuals want to be leaders, not followers.

Was the person born under the zodiac sign Virgo?

Practical and unassuming, Virgos want to be useful. In both their personal and professional lives, they are efficient, orderly, and attentive to details. These shy, sensitive, and kind individuals enjoy helping other people.

Was the person born under the zodiac sign Libra?

Sociable Libras enjoy the company of other people and excel at relationships of all kinds. They love beauty in all its forms and many of them possess artistic ability of some kind. Peace-loving Libras try to avoid controversy and arguments.

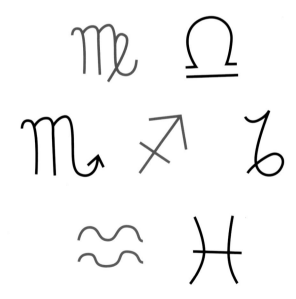

Was the person born under the zodiac sign Scorpio?

Shrewd, insightful Scorpios are very private people and prefer to be "the power behind the throne," so to speak. Sensitive and emotional, they need to feel they are in control of things. Nothing deters them once they decide to do something.

Was the person born under the zodiac sign Sagittarius?

Sagittarians are idealists and visionaries, but often lack the persistence to bring their dreams to fruition. These restless people love to travel. Gregarious and optimistic, they have a good sense of humor and attract many friends.

Was the person born under the zodiac sign Capricorn?

Capricorns are determined, responsible, and pragmatic, so they often excel in business. Conservative and cautious, they respect traditions and dislike change. Although they appear cold on the outside, they are really quite sensitive.

Was the person born under the zodiac sign Aquarius?

These free-spirited people rebel against rules and conventions and enjoy being "different." Always in the vanguard, they are innovators who seek change and new experiences. Their outgoing, offbeat personalities attract friends and associates of all kinds.

Was the person born under the zodiac sign Pisces?

Pisces people are sensitive, intuitive, and reclusive—these dreamers don't seem to live in the "real world." They have wonderful imaginations and are often artists, musicians, or poets. Kind and compassionate, they enjoy helping others.

Examine a person's signature.

If someone writes his or her name with large, bold letters, that person is gregarious and enjoys attention. A small signature suggests someone who is reclusive and doesn't want to attract attention. (For more information about handwriting analysis, see Chapter 3.)

Look at the initials in a person's signature.

If the initials in a person's signature are much larger than the rest of the letters in the name, he or she seeks recognition. This individual may present a strong image, but probably lacks self-confidence.

Check the ascending strokes in a person's handwriting.

If the ascending strokes in a person's handwriting are very tall, he or she tends to be an idea person.

Check the descending strokes in a person's handwriting.

If the descending strokes are long, the person is practical and well grounded in the physical world. If the descenders also have large loops, the person enjoys sensual pleasures.

Notice the spaces between words.

Large spaces between words in a person's handwriting suggest that he or she is daring and imaginative. If the words are closely spaced, the writer is cautious and conservative.

Look at the loops in a person's handwriting.

Narrow or closed loops suggest that the person is secretive, defensive, or shy.
Large loops indicate that the writer is open and trusting.

Examine the slant of a person's handwriting.

The more a person's letters slant to the right, the more emotional he or she
is. Straight up-and-down letters signify a controlled, pragmatic individual.
If the letters slant backward (to the left), the person is guarded and fearful
of revealing him- or herself.

Look at a photo of a stranger.

Ask a friend to show you a photograph of a person he or she knows, but you have never met. As you gaze at the photo, allow your intuition to tell you about this individual. Check with your friend to see how much of the information you picked up psychically is correct.

Ask a friend to pick a rune.

Let a friend mix up a set of runes, then select one without looking at it. This rune will describe an issue or situation that is in the forefront of your friend's mind. Refer to Chapter 3 for an interpretation of the rune chosen.

Ask a friend to pick a tarot card.

Let your friend shuffle the cards from the major arcana of the tarot and, without looking, choose one card. This describes an issue or situation that is in the forefront of your friend's mind. Chapter 3 gives brief interpretations of the cards to help you understand what's going on in your friend's life and how he or she can best proceed.

Ask a friend to draw a picture of a house.

Houses symbolize our lives. Ask a friend to draw a picture of an imaginary house (not an architectural rendering of his or her own or someone else's house). Notice the house's condition, size, shape, color, relationship to other buildings, and so forth. Think of the windows as "eyes" and the door as a "mouth." What does this picture tell you about your friend?

Read someone's tea leaves.

Although reading tea leaves proficiently requires some study, you can glean information intuitively by gazing at the pattern of the leaves in the bottom of a cup. Brew a cup of loose tea for another person. After he or she has drunk the tea, empty out any remaining liquid, leaving the wet leaves clinging to the cup. What does the configuration tell you?

Create a sigil from a friend's name.

A sigil is a secret symbol that contains letters, numbers, and/or images interwoven to create a picture. It is secret because no one but you can read it. Write the letters of a friend's name, then configure them in various ways until you arrive at a design you like. You can draw the letters in any arrangement—upside-down, backward, both uppercase and lower—so long as you include all the letters. When you have finished, look at the image—it presents a new way of viewing this person. What does it tell you about your friend? What does it tell you about your relationship with him or her? If you wish to, give the sigil to your friend as a talisman.

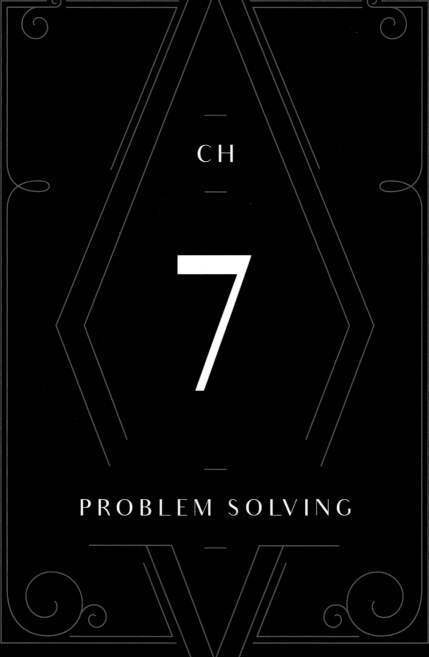

CH

7

PROBLEM SOLVING

Entrepreneur Paul Hawken said, "A problem is an opportunity in drag." Problems are absolutely necessary for our continued growth—they are the bridges by which we cross from innocence to understanding.

Some problems can't be solved using everyday, rational, left-brain thinking. Sometimes we need to think "outside the box" in order to solve conundrums that defy logic.

Many famous people who could hardly be called "flakes"—Albert Einstein, Jonas Salk, Ben Franklin, and Franklin Roosevelt among them—relied on their intuition to help them solve problems and handle challenges in their lives. Salk, who created a vaccine for polio, even wrote a book on intuition in which he suggested that creativity arises from the interaction of intuition and reason.

Our "inner wisdom" knows the answers to every dilemma, not only those facing us right now, but those we will encounter in the future. In some cases, we know deep down how to resolve a perplexing situation, but can't seem to retrieve the information from the subconscious. As a schoolgirl, I discovered that if I wasn't sure of an answer to a test question, I had a good chance of getting it right anyway if I simply wrote down the first thing that popped into my head. But if I thought about it too much, then went back and changed my first "guess," the second answer was usually wrong.

In other instances, the solution exists in the etheric web—that cosmic library some metaphysicians call the Akasic Records—and we can use our psychic powers to access it. That's what Edgar Cayce did when he retrieved ancient wisdom from distant sources while he slept. All we need to do is trust that an answer exists and that it will be presented to us at the right time.

Divination tools, including tarot cards, runes, the *I Ching*, and the pendulum, serve as catalysts to problem solving. They connect us with our own subconscious minds and provide a road map to the unseen realms where higher knowledge awaits us. Prayer, meditation, chanting, and other practices provide nonrational means for gaining assistance from sources outside our ordinary mental functioning. The techniques in this chapter are designed to help you use your ESP to dip into that bottomless well of wisdom for the answers to problems both large and small.

Ask for help.

Unless you ask for help, you may not receive it. Think of your inner wisdom as a good friend who is always willing to lend a hand if you request it.

Expect to receive help.

Keep an open mind—doubt interferes with success in all endeavors. Believe that if you seek help, you will receive it.

When you are ready, a solution will appear.

There is a saying in some spiritual traditions that when the student is ready, the teacher will appear. This is also true of problems. When you are ready to accept advice from your intuition or a higher source and are willing to deal with your problem, a solution will present itself to you.

Don't second-guess the help you receive.

If you ask for help and receive intuitive advice that you don't like— from an oracle, a dream, or some other source—don't discount it and continue asking in the hope that you'll get another answer that you'll prefer. Accept and work to the best of your ability with the information you've been given.

Express gratitude for help received.

If a person helped you out of a difficult situation, you'd thank him or her, right? If you receive assistance from a higher source or your own inner knowing, shouldn't you thank whomever or whatever provided that help? Doing so encourages the source of that help to continue offering assistance.

Don't focus on your problem.

When you focus on something, you increase its power and its impact in your life. The *I Ching* recommends turning your attention away from the problem to diminish its importance while trusting that it will be resolved.

Make a list of possible solutions.

Make a list of possible solutions to your problem. Relax your mind as you do this, rather than concentrating too hard on the process. You are priming the pump, so to speak, inviting your subconscious and your higher knowledge to present you with options your rational mind hasn't considered yet.

Sleep on it.

Many famous people have taken this approach to problem solving. When you go to bed at night, ask your subconscious and your higher self to help you resolve your dilemma while you sleep.

Stare into a candle's flame.

Think of a question you'd like answered or a situation about which you want information. In a darkened room, light a candle and gaze into the flame. Relax your mind and allow images to slowly arise into your consciousness. The impressions you receive will shed light on the question or situation.

Open a book to a random page.

Select a book containing spiritual guidance (the *Bible*, *Torah*, *Koran*, or *Tao Te Ching*, for example) or one by a wise man or woman, such as the writings of the Sufi poet Rumi. Even respected literary works like those of Shakespeare will work. Think or ask your question aloud. Then open the book at random and place your finger on the page without looking. Read the passage you selected to gain insight into your problem.

Write an affirmation.

An affirmation is a short, positive statement you create to retrain your subconscious. If you are seeking a new job, for instance, write an affirmation such as "I now have the perfect job." Display this written affirmation in a place where you will see it often.

Walk a labyrinth.

If possible, walk through a full-size labyrinth. If that's not an option, trace the black lines in this diagram with a pointed object. Relax your mind and focus your attention on your movement along the labyrinth's winding pathways, into the center and back out again. As you shift directions, you alternate between using the right brain and the left brain, activating both hemispheres to find an answer to your problem.

Chant.

Chanting is a way of sending a message into the energy matrix of our universe to ask for something you want. The repetitive sounds produce vibrations that attract your request.

Pray.

Like chanting, praying sends a request for help to your higher self and/or other forces in the universe. (Studies have shown that praying can actually produce miracles.)

Burn incense.

In some spiritual traditions, incense is used as an adjunct to prayer, meditation, and chanting. The smoke from the burning incense carries your requests to deities in the higher planes.

Flip a coin.

Although this may sound trite, flipping a coin can be a reasonable way to get an answer to a question. As with more complex oracles, this method is a way of connecting with your "inner knowing." "Heads" means the answer to your question is yes; "tails," the answer is no.

Toss three coins.

For information about a problem, ask a question that can be answered with yes or no. Toss three coins onto a table or other surface. If two or three coins fall heads up, the answer is yes. If two or three coins fall tails up, the answer is no.

Smell lavender essential oil.

Lavender helps quiet your nerves. Rub a little lavender essential oil on your wrist and sniff it to reduce stress.

Smell peppermint essential oil.

Peppermint stimulates the mind and encourages mental clarity. Rub a little peppermint essential oil on your wrist and sniff it while thinking about your problem. The fragrance will help clear your mind so you can arrive at a solution.

Smell lemon essential oil.

Like peppermint, the fresh clean scent of lemon clears and stimulates the mind. Rub a little lemon essential oil on your wrist and sniff it while thinking about your problem. The fragrance will help clear your mind so your intuition can offer a solution.

Drink a peppermint or lemon infusion.

If you prefer, you can put a drop or two of peppermint or lemon essential oil in a glass of water and drink it to open your mind and stimulate your intuition.

Burn a green candle to attract money.

Green is associated with growth. It is also the color of paper money in some countries. If you have financial problems, use a nail to scratch the word "prosperity" into a green votive candle. Place the candle in a safe place and let it burn completely.

Burn a pink candle to attract love.

Pink is the color of love. If you want to attract a new love relationship or improve an existing one, use a nail to scratch the word "love" into a pink votive candle. Place the candle in a safe place and allow it to burn completely.

Play word association with a friend.

Ask a friend to toss out words that relate to your problem, such as "debt" or "stress" or "loneliness." Respond quickly, without giving it much conscious thought, with the first word that pops into your head. Keep doing this, and soon some interesting ideas will arise from your inner wisdom to help you understand and solve your problem.

Find a convenient parking space.

When you are still several blocks away from your destination, clearly visualize an empty space right where you want to park. Once you become adept at this psychic skill, you won't waste time driving around city streets or a crowded shopping mall.

Choose a door.

Remember that TV game show *Let's Make a Deal?* Relax, close your eyes, and imagine three closed doors before you. An answer to your problem waits behind each door. Pick the one that offers the best solution.

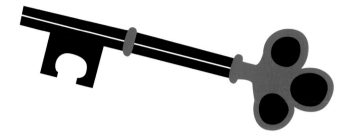

Find the key to unlock a problem.

Choose a key—an old, decorative one is best—and assign it the task of unlocking problem situations. Form a picture in your imagination of slipping the key into a lock, which symbolizes your problem, and opening it. Wear this key or carry it on your key ring to help unlock any problems you might encounter.

Find a lost pet.

Animals are very sensitive to psychic communication. If your pet is lost, bring him or her home by sending a mental message. Relax, close your eyes, and bring the pet's image into your mind. In your mind's eye, see your pet walking up to your door. Think or say, "[Pet's name] is now home, safe and sound."

Change the way you write your t's.

If you want to be more successful, cross your t's higher on the stem. A low cross stoke signifies low expectations; a high cross stroke shows you are striving for greatness. Be sure the cross stroke touches the upright stroke, however, or your dreams may be out of reach. (For more information about handwriting, see Chapter 3.)

Change the way you dot your i's.

If you want to become more grounded and realistic, dot your i's closer to the stem. A dot that is written directly above and close to the upright stroke indicates conscientiousness, practicality, and attention to detail; a dot that is far removed from the stem suggests an overly idealistic and "spacey" attitude.

Change your handwriting to stimulate insights and ideas.

The ascending strokes in your handwriting describe your mental processes. Intentionally make the ascenders longer to help you increase your insight and stimulate ideas.

Change your handwriting to increase practicality.

The descending strokes in your handwriting describe your relationship to the physical world. Intentionally make the descenders longer to help you stay grounded and become more practical.

Change your handwriting to save money.

If you are trying to save money, use smaller left and right margins when you write. By filling up more of the page, you show that you want to be thriftier and more efficient at handling money.

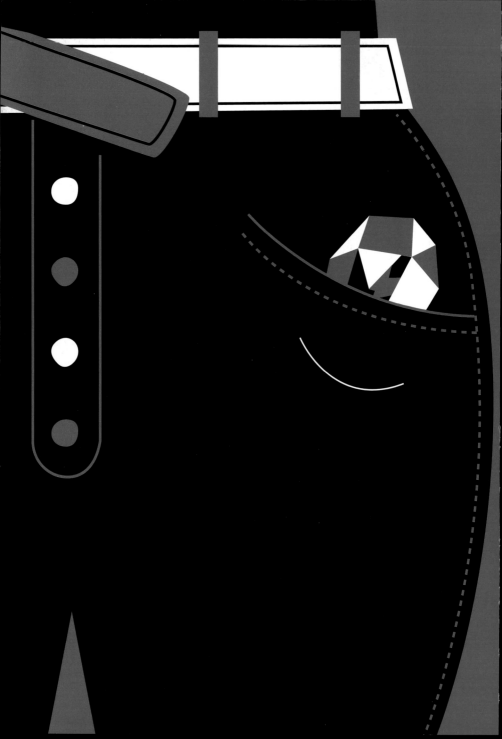

Program a crystal.

Quartz crystals hold information and can be programmed with your objective. Cleanse the crystal by holding it under running water for a minute or so. Then hold the crystal to your forehead while you ask it to help you resolve the problem.

Carry a piece of rose quartz in your pocket.

Rose quartz is associated with love and contentment. Carry a piece of rose quartz in your pocket to attract love into your life. Whenever you touch it, you'll be reminded of your intention and your thoughts will send out positive vibrations to a potential partner.

Carry a piece of amethyst in your pocket.

Amethyst is associated with peace of mind and relaxation. To reduce stress, carry a smoothly tumbled piece of amethyst in your pocket. Each time you touch it, you'll be reminded of your intention to stay calm.

Wear amber for protection.

Whenever you feel the need for a little extra protection, wear amber jewelry or carry a piece of amber in your pocket.

Pick a card from the major arcana.

Separate the major arcana cards from the deck. Shuffle these twenty-two cards while you think about your question. Ask for advice, then select a card. Refer to the list in Chapter 3 to see what the card you drew means—or, look up its interpretation in a book about the tarot.

Use playing cards to get an answer.

Shuffle a deck of regular playing cards while you think about your problem. Then, ask a yes-or-no question. Begin turning cards face up, one by one, in a pile. If you turn up an ace before you count out thirteen cards, stop and begin a new pile. If you count out thirteen cards without turning up an ace, stop and begin a new pile. Make three piles of cards in this manner. If you turned over two or three aces and the symbols of the suits are upright, your answer is yes. If you turned over two or three aces and the symbols are upside down, your answer is no. If you turned up only one ace or none, an answer cannot be determined yet. If one ace is upright and the other is upside down, the situation is still in flux and your actions could affect the outcome. (Note: Before shuffling, find the ace of diamonds in the deck and mark the "bottom" of the card so you'll know whether it's upright or upside down.)

Ask for guidance in your dreams.

Before you go to sleep, ask your subconscious to send you help and guidance in your dreams.

Pay attention to dreams about cars.

In dreams, cars symbolize your actions. The next time you dream about being in a car, notice who is driving—is someone else at the wheel while you go along for the ride? Shift into the driver's seat and take charge of your problems.

Burn your problem.

Write down your problem on a piece of paper. Then, burn the piece of paper. As the paper turns to ash, envision your problem disappearing.

Give your home a psychic housecleaning.

A house holds on to the emotional energy of its inhabitants. After an argument or crisis, give your home a psychic housecleaning to get rid of unwanted vibrations that may be disturbing your peace. Use a real broom—or simply imagine one in your mind's eye—to sweep the air in each room until you've "cleared the air" throughout.

Get rid of someone else's psychic energy.

When you move into a new home, visualize white light filling the entire space to purify and protect it. This technique psychically clears the previous inhabitants' energy from your home.

Select a rune.

Mix up the runes in your set while you think about your problem. Ask for advice in a yes-or-no question, then select one rune without looking. Refer to Chapter 3 to see what the rune you picked means—or, look up its interpretation in a book about the runes.

Select three runes.

Mix up the runes in your set while you think about your problem. Ask for advice in a yes-or-no question, then select three runes without looking. Toss them gently onto a tabletop or other surface. If two or three runes fall right-side up, your answer is yes. If two or three fall upside down, your answer is no. Also check Chapter 3 or a good book on runes to see what each of the runes you selected means.

Use a pendulum to advise you.

Hold a pendulum loosely between your thumb and index finger. Ask it if you should take a certain action regarding a problem. The pendulum will swing from side to side if the answer is no. If the answer is yes, the pendulum will swing back and forth. (For more about pendulums, see Chapter 3.)

Use the pendulum to learn about someone else.

Hold a pendulum loosely between your thumb and index finger. Ask about someone you are having a problem with. The pendulum will swing in a clockwise circle if the overall situation is favorable or the outcome looks good. The pendulum will swing in a counterclockwise circle if the overall situation isn't to your advantage or the outcome doesn't look promising.

Find lost objects with a pendulum.

If you misplace something in your home, hold a pendulum over a floor plan of your house or apartment. As you hold the pendulum above each room or area, ask, "Is it here?" The pendulum will swing from side to side if the answer is no. If the answer is yes, the pendulum will swing back and forth.

Heal an injury with green light.

Green is the color of health. If you have an injury, close your eyes and imagine green light surrounding and infusing the injured part. Hold this image in your mind for as long as possible. Do this several times a day to help the injury heal more quickly.

Protect yourself with white light.

White is the color of protection. When you feel the need for a little extra protection, close your eyes and imagine that your entire body is surrounded by a cocoon of pure white light. Think or say, "I am protected by pure white light; nothing can harm me."

Protect someone else with white light.

If someone you know may be in danger or needs additional protection while traveling, for instance, send him or her white light. As above, envision the person wrapped in a cocoon of pure white light while you think or say aloud, "[Name] is protected by pure white light, nothing can harm [him or her]."

Improve your sense of security with red light.

At the base of your spine is the "root chakra," which is linked to your sense of security. If you are feeling insecure, close your eyes and visualize a ball of clear red light glowing here. Feel its warmth. This activates the chakra and enhances your sense of security and personal power.

Change an unpleasant situation with pink light.

Pink is the color of love and joy. You can change an unpleasant situation by visualizing the space around you being filled with pink light. If another person is the source of your discomfort due to a disagreement, for example, also envision him or her and the space between you bathed in pink light.

Reduce stress in your environment with blue light.

Blue is a calming, soothing color that has clinically been shown to reduce tension. If you are in a stressful environment, such as a busy office, visualize the space being filled with true blue light.

Increase your self-confidence with purple light.

Purple is the color of wisdom, so this technique works well when you are about to speak in front of a group, go to a job interview, or face a challenging situation that you feel insecure about. Envision your entire body surrounded by purple light—the reddish purple tones, such as fuchsia or magenta, are best.

Breathe deeply.

Often the answer to a problem lies just below the surface of your consciousness. Take several slow, deep breaths and allow yourself to relax mentally as well as physically. Focus on your breathing, not on the problem. You'll gradually receive insights that can help you handle the problem.

Picture yourself thin.

If you are trying to lose weight, cut from a magazine a picture of a body that looks the way you want yours to look. Then, cut your face from a photograph and paste it on the body. Display the composite image on your mirror. The picture has a positive impact on your subconscious and helps to stimulate weight loss.

Go with the flow.

Do you feel like your problem is a river and you are swimming upstream? Close your eyes and envision yourself turning over onto your back. Relax and let yourself "go with the flow" rather than struggle. As you float comfortably on your back, allow your intuition to present a solution to you.

Use pictures to improve your finances.

Cut from magazines pictures that represent prosperity to you. Display them in a place where you will see them often. These images help you "put the word out" to the universe and draw riches to you.

Tap the power of words to improve your health.

Words, like pictures, can be used to change unwanted conditions and attract situations you desire. Write the words "good health" in green letters and display them on your refrigerator door. Each time you see the words, you'll be reminded of your intention to eat healthy food and improve your physical well-being.

Use acupressure to improve your memory.

If you have problems concentrating or remembering things, close your eyes and gently press with the tip of one finger the point between your nose and upper lip. Hold this for about thirty seconds to help you focus your mind or recall something.

Use acupressure to reduce stress.

Close your eyes and gently press your fingertips to your temples for thirty seconds to help reduce tension.

Carry the rune *Gifu* in your pocket to attract love.

This rune is connected with love. To attract a new partner or to improve an existing relationship, carry the symbol above in your pocket. Touch it often to reaffirm your desire to increase the love in your life.

Display the rune *Fehu* in your workplace.

This rune signifies financial gain and fortunate career opportunities. Place the symbol above in a prominent place where you will see it often. Each time you look at it, you'll reinforce your intention to improve your work situation and send out psychic vibes that will make these wishes come true.

Display the Strength tarot card to bolster your courage.
In many decks, this card depicts a young woman holding the jaws of a
lion. The image represents one gaining power over fear, ego, desire, and
other emotions or attitudes that may be interfering with success. Place
this card where you will see it often and let it help you gain courage to do
what needs to be done.

**Contemplate the Emperor tarot card to improve your financial
management skills.**
This card represents financial mastery and success in the material world.
Spend a few moments each day gazing at this card. Let it impress its
energy and symbolism on your subconscious in order to help you find
ways to manage your money better and improve your financial situation.

Contemplate the Lovers tarot card to increase the love in your life.
This card depicts a happy couple and its message is clear. Gaze at it
to attract a new lover or improve an existing relationship. Each time
you look at it, you'll send out loving vibrations that your partner will
intuitively feel.

Focus on the Wheel of Fortune tarot card to attract good luck.
This card represents being in the right place at the right time and signals
a time when your luck changes for the better. If you've been experiencing
a run of bad luck, focus your attention on this card several times a day. Its
symbolism will influence your subconscious and help you to intuitively
position yourself to receive good fortune.

Ask the *I Ching* for advice.

Ask a question, then toss three coins together six times, making sure
to note how the coins fall (heads or tails up). Draw a hexagram that
corresponds to your coin tosses—two or three heads are symbolized by a
solid line, two or three tails by a broken line. Draw the hexagram from the
bottom up. Consult a good book on the *I Ching* for an interpretation.

Display the *I Ching* hexagram *T'ai* to dissolve tension.

If you are experiencing stress or are at odds with another person, this
image, which means "peace," can help dissolve tension. Draw the
hexagram above on a piece of paper and display it where you will see it
often. Each time you gaze at the image, you'll feel a sense of calm.

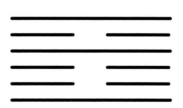

Display the hexagram *Ta Yu* to improve finances.

Translated, this hexagram means "possession in great measure," and it can help you attract prosperity. Draw the image above on a piece of paper and display it in a prominent place. Each time you look at it, you'll be reminded of your intention to improve your finances.

Display the hexagram *Shih Ho* to help you overcome an obstacle.

This hexagram means "biting through" in English and can help give you the determination to overcome an obstacle. Draw the image above on a piece of paper and display it in a prominent place. Each time you look at it, you'll strengthen your resolve and elicit the aid of your intuition.

Change the way you think about someone.

Other people sense how you think and feel about them, even if you don't display it outwardly. If you want to change how another person behaves toward you, you must first change your own attitudes about that person. For instance, focus on his or her positive qualities rather than the negative ones. Or, as the *I Ching* advises, try to see the "god-being" within that person, rather than only the "ego-being" on the outside.

Change the feeling a situation elicits in you.

Your emotional energy creates vibrations in your environment and, when negative, can exacerbate a difficult situation. If you are involved in an argument with someone, for example, take a few deep breaths, then reach down inside yourself to find feelings of happiness, peace, or love. Focus on feeling and emitting these emotions, rather than anger, in order to defuse the situation.

Draw a picture that symbolizes your problem.

Encapsulate a problem in a symbolic form. Make a simple line drawing that represents your feelings about a problem. For example, a box might mean you feel closed in; a flat line could symbolize boredom; a knot may stand for tangled emotions. Contemplate your drawing to discover other things it says to you about resolving the problem.

Take flower essences to increase self-confidence.

Dr. Edward Bach discovered that ingesting a few drops daily of the distilled essence of the cones of the larch tree could increase self-confidence. Bach flower remedies can be purchased in most health-food stores.

Take flower essences to restore hope.

According to Dr. Bach, ingesting the essence of sweet chestnut can help you release old hurts and regain hope for the future.

Take flower essences to find your purpose in life.

Taking a few drops daily of the Bach flower remedy Wild Oat can help you discover your purpose in life and improve your ability to pursue meaningful goals.

Eat asparagus to increase your good fortune.
Asparagus is linked with expansiveness and opportunity. Eating it regularly helps you keep a positive outlook, thereby improving your chances in life.

Eat chocolate to increase your love quotient.
Physically, chocolate stimulates the production of endorphins in the brain, which increases loving feelings. Eating chocolate can help you send out loving vibrations to attract a new partner or improve an existing relationship. (Note: This may work better for women than for men due to differences in brain chemistry.)

Eat apricots to improve your love life.
If you can't eat chocolate, substitute apricots to improve your love life. Apricots are said to be the fruit of Venus, the goddess of love.

Create a psychic haven.

We all need a place to retreat to when things get too stressful. In your mind's eye, create a peaceful, beautiful haven you can go to when you want or need to. This is your private "psychic sanctuary" and you can go there in your imagination whenever you wish.

Massage your feet to reduce tension.

Reflexology is the healing art of foot massage, a therapy that has been practiced at least since the time of ancient Egypt. Each part of the sole is linked with another part of the body. Massage your feet, applying gentle pressure, to reduce stress. If any spots feel tender, give them a little special attention, gradually working out the "kinks."

Listen to the expressions you use.

Notice the common expressions you use in everyday speech—they often provide clues about physical ailments and other problems in your life that may be related. Is something or someone giving you a "pain in the neck?" Do you find a situation "hard to stomach?" Try to change the unpleasant situation before it materializes as a physical ailment.

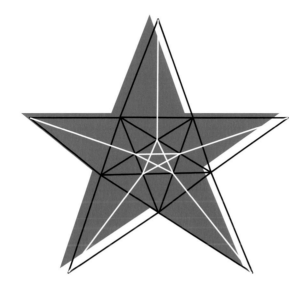

Use a star to protect yourself.

The star is a symbol of protection (sheriffs used to wear badges shaped like stars over their hearts). Stand with your arms held straight out at your sides and spread your legs about two feet apart, so that your body resembles a star. Close your eyes and envision a blue star superimposed over your body. This star will protect you from harm.

Erase a problem.

On a blackboard, write down the problem that you want to eliminate. Use an eraser to wipe the slate clean. If you don't have access to a blackboard, you can write your problem in the dirt, then rub it out. The visual impact of this action will imprint itself on your psyche and help you erase the problem from your life.

Store a problem in a piece of smoky quartz.

One of the most notable characteristics of quartz is its memory—it's even used in computers to store information. Smoky quartz will keep a problem "on ice" for you until you are ready to deal with it. Hold the crystal to your forehead or heart and release your problem into the quartz for safekeeping. At a later date, when you are ready, you can retrieve the problem and resolve it.

Give a problem a name.

When you name something, you take control of it and put it in perspective. Give a name to a problem you are struggling with—it can be a name that succinctly describes the situation, a humorous name, or one that has personal significance for you. In doing so, you objectify the problem so you can detach your emotions and ego from it. The problem becomes a separate entity—like a child, an animal, or an employee—that you can confront and manage.

Go for a walk.

Take a walk alone in a peaceful place. Allow your conscious mind to relax as you enjoy the serene environment. This lets your intuitive processes take over and provide a solution to your problem.

Take a drive.

Driving on the highway or a familiar road often puts you in a light trance in which you are alert but not relying totally on your rational thinking processes. While in this state of mind, your intuition can come to the fore and offer suggestions for solving your problem.

Get help from the north.
North is the direction that relates to practical, physical matters. If your problem involves money or material concerns, face north, close your eyes, and envision help flowing to you from this direction.

Get help from the south.
South is the direction that relates to vitality and enthusiasm. If you feel lethargic, dispirited, or discouraged about something, face south, close your eyes, and envision help flowing to you from this direction.

Get help from the east.
East is the direction that relates to ideas and communication. If you are experiencing problems involving communication or need inspiration, face east, close your eyes, and envision help flowing to you from this direction.

Get help from the west.
West is the direction that relates to emotions and relationships. If you are experiencing problems in these areas, face west, close your eyes, and envision help flowing to you from this direction.

Cure hiccups.

The next time you have hiccups, relax, close your eyes, and take a deep breath. Inhale slowly to a count of four, then hold your breath to a count of four, then release the breath to a count of four. Repeat this three times if necessary. Yogis consider the breath to contain the essence of life, having psychic as well as physical healing properties.

Write a story with a happy ending.

Use your imagination and intuition to give a problem a happy ending. Write a short story in which the situation turns out favorably for all concerned. Don't worry about the quality or style of your writing. By creating this vision, you inform the psychic web of the outcome you desire.

Draw a picture of what you want.

Sketch an image that depicts the resolution you desire for a problematic situation. Don't try to be Michelangelo, just create a positive impression. This action sends a message into the psychic web and helps to generate the outcome you want.

Don't give up hope.

If you give up on the possibility of solving a problem, you may never succeed. Continue to believe that a solution exists and allow your intuition to keep presenting potential answers to your dilemma. In time, the right answer will appear.

Resources

Alexander, Skye, *10-Minute Feng Shui* (Gloucester, Massachusetts: Fair Winds Press, 2002).

Alexander, Skye, *Planets in Signs* (West Chester, Pennsylvania: Whitford Press/Schiffer Publishing, 1988).

Bluestone, Sarvananda, *How to Read Signs and Omens in Everyday Life* (Rochester, Vermont: Destiny Books, 2002), pp. xiv, 17, 55, 67.

Branston, Barry, *The Elements of Graphology* (Rockport, Massachusetts: Element Books, 1995), pp. 3–4.

Hawken, Paul, *Growing a Business* (New York: Simon & Schuster, 1987), p. 37.

Salk, Jonas, *Anatomy of Reality: Merging of Intuition and Reason* (New York: Columbia University Press, 1983).

Schulz, Mona Lisa, *Awakening Intuition* (New York: Three Rivers Press, 1999), p. 30.

About the Author

S kye Alexander is the author of more than forty fiction
and nonfiction books. Her stories have been published
in anthologies internationally and her work has been
translated into more than a dozen languages. She is also an
artist, astrologer, tarot reader, and feng shui practitioner.

Visit her at www.skyealexander.com.

INDEX